Foreign language learning in primary schools (age 5/6 to 10/11)

edited by

Peter Doyé
Technische Universität Braunschweig, Germany

Alison Hurrell
Northern College of Education, Aberdeen, Scotland

Education Committee
Council for Cultural Co-operation

Council of Europe Publishing

French edition:

L'enseignement des langues à l'école primaire

ISBN 92-871-3249-6

The opinions expressed in this work are those of the authors and do not necessarily reflect the official policy of the Council for Cultural Co-operation of the Council of Europe.

All correspondence concerning this publication or the reproduction or translation of all or part of the document should be addressed to the Director of Education, Culture and Sport of the Council of Europe (F-67075 Strasbourg Cedex).

The reproduction of extracts is authorised, except for commercial purposes, on condition that the source is quoted.

Council of Europe Publishing
F-67075 Strasbourg Cedex

ISBN 92-871-3242-9
© Council of Europe, 1997
Printed in Germany

TABLE OF CONTENTS

PREFACE

When launching the Council of Europe Modern Languages Project: *'Language learning for European citizenship'* the Education Committee identified a number of educational sectors and themes for priority treatment. In the course of the Project, which was conducted between 1989 and 1996, work in these areas was intensively pursued, partly by studies commissioned from leading experts in the field, but mainly in a series of 'new-style' workshops, attended by colleagues professionally active in the fields concerned. These were nominated by member governments and worked together under the leadership of 'animators' selected by the Council of Europe from among the acknowledged leading experts in Europe.

A 'new-style' workshop was held on the initiative of two co-operating member countries to deal with a theme identified by them as of particular importance. Each 'new-style' workshop had three phases. First, an initiating workshop of some five days' duration was held on the invitation of one member government. Here the aim was to establish the 'state of the art' in the sector or with regard to the theme, to identify areas in which further research and development work was needed, and then to set up an 'action programme' of projects to be carried out by individuals or institutions in two or more member countries under a project co-ordinator. In a second phase, this action programme was then conducted, normally over a two-year period, during which two Progress Reports on the conduct of the Projects were published. In a third phase, the outcomes of the Projects were reported by the Co-ordinators to a follow-up workshop, hosted by the second co-operating member government. Following the discussion of the projects and their products, the workshop concluded by setting out conclusions and recommendations regarding the general development of the field and future policy orientations.

Many of the new-style workshops have dealt with more than one priority sector or theme, and some themes to which a number of governments attached importance were the subjects of a number of workshops. As a result, contributions relating to particular priority sectors and themes were spread over a number of workshop reports, progress reports and independent studies. In addition, constraints on workshop time and report space have placed strict limits on the animators' introductions to workshop themes. The Council of Europe has therefore decided to commission a series of Compendia, each of which would bring together a number of the more significant contributions made to the Project in respect of one of its major areas of concern. In a number of cases this meant leaving aside a number of valuable contributions for which room could not be found in the agreed format, especially since authors have been given the opportunity to develop and up-date their contributions.

The teaching of modern languages to young children has been one of the focal points of the Project. Language provision in primary schools varies very widely across Europe.

This is partly because school systems differ in the age at which compulsory education begins, and the terms used to label different forms and stages of earlier education. Again, the age of transition from primary to secondary education varies. Overall, we may be speaking of a sector which starts somewhere between 4 and 7 and ends between 8 and 15. Different interfaces may be present at age 6, 8, 10, 11, 12, 14 or 15 according to the particular national systems concerned. Some countries (e.g. UK) maintain a number of different systems side-by-side. Accordingly, generalisations are hard to make and the question whether foreign languages should or should not be introduced into primary education may mean very different things according to the age-range of the children affected. In 1961, the Second Conference of European Ministers of Eduction in Hamburg requested the Council of Europe to investigate the advisability of an early start to language learning. Since that time expert opinion has been divided, initially polarised between those who believed that first language development would be damaged by the learning of a second language and others who held that there was a 'critical period' during which the plasticity of the young brain uniquely favoured language acquisition. Research (and experience) has not confirmed either position. Plurilingualism has been found to facilitate rather than disrupt the development of the mother tongue. In most respects, however, older learners appear to be more efficient than younger learners (except in respect of the 'naturalness' of speech). The issues are not, however, closed.

In practice, national attitudes to early learning are a fairly sensitive indicator of the value placed on foreign language proficiency in the society concerned. Where proficiency in one or more foreign languages is felt to be essential to proper career development, parental pressure for an early start is very strong. If schools in the state education system do not provide it, or are not thought to be very effective, parents will pay for private teaching. A parallel system of out-of-school provision may develop and place increasing pressure on state provision. Where foreign language proficiency is not highly valued, however, curricular space is restricted, plurilingualism is resisted and the lowering of the starting age is held to be impracticable and a waste of resources.

Inevitably, as the importance of foreign language proficiency has grown - and been seen to grow - in response to the revolution in communications and information technology and its impact on all aspects of modern living, continent-wide pressure for an earlier start has grown. It is not surprising that five member countries, UK (Scotland), France, Germany, Austria and Spain have offered workshops in this area and that the R&D projects carried out in inter-workshop action programmes have produced interesting and valuable results. The workshops, in one or other of which almost all member states were represented, have come firmly and unanimously to the conclusion that the lowering of the starting age is, educationally both desirable and feasible. The papers collected here by Peter Doyé and Alison Hurrell, both of whom played a valuable part in the series of workshops, will give some of the evidence on which this conclusion is based and will, we trust, be of practical help to practitioners in the field.

John L.M. TRIM, Project Director

6

INTRODUCTION
Peter DOYÉ and Alison HURRELL

1. The European Context

From its inception, the Council for Cultural Cooperation (CDCC) has been concerned with the promotion of foreign language learning in its member states and has tried to support national initiatives for the improvement of foreign language education. In the 1980s an extensive project entitled "Learning and teaching modern languages for communication" (Project N°12) was conducted and produced valuable results. From 1982 to 1988 a series of international workshops were held, where the key areas were lower secondary education, adult education and the education of migrants. At its 55th Session in January 1989, the CDCC, reviewing the outcomes of Project N°12, noted the encouraging progress which had been made, but also stressed the need to continue the process of reform. Above all, this process was to include further sectors of education and to treat further issues felt to be necessary components of a conceptual framework for the learning and teaching of foreign languages in Europe.

The new **sectors** were
- primary education
- upper secondary education
- advanced adult education and
- vocationally oriented education

The priority **themes** were
- the specification of objectives;
- the use of mass media and new technologies;
- bilingual education;
- the educational exploitation of visits and exchanges;
- the preparation of pupils and students for independent learning;
- appropriate methods and procedures for assessment and evaluation;

In order to cover these sectors and themes the CDCC launched a new project called "Language Learning for European Citizenship" which had as its main purpose the extension of the work done so far to the above mentioned sectors and themes.

It was through this new project that Foreign Language Education in Primary Schools became a priority area of the CDCC.

Five workshops were dedicated to this area:

Workshop 4A in June 1991 in Scotland
Workshop 8A in May 1992 in Germany
Workshop 4B in December 1993 in France

Workshop 8B in May 1995 in Austria
Workshop 17 in September 1995 in Spain

Each of these workshops considered the whole spectrum of early foreign language education, but placed special emphasis on different aspects of this education. It seemed desirable, therefore, to integrate the results of the discussions, investigations and reflections of all five workshops and to attempt a synopsis of the relevant issues.

For this purpose, the Council for Cultural Cooperation commissioned a compendium which might serve as a source of information for all European teachers, teacher trainers and curriculum developers in the field. The CDCC entrusted the editors of this book with the preparation, coordination and publication of such a compendium.

The aims of the compendium are

1. to analyse the results of the work of the international workshops and of the related research and development programmes concerning the priority sector 'Primary Education' and

2. to identify the main aspects, trends, theoretical approaches and innovative teaching practices by means of individual contributions describing theoretical and practical developments.

The central part of this book consists of six chapters on the six most important aspects of foreign language education in primary schools as they emerged out of the work of the five workshops listed above and because they seemed to be the logical components of this education.

The six aspects are treated in one chapter each:

1. Objectives and contents
2. Methods
3. Resources
4. Organisation, Integration, Continuity
5. Evaluation and Assessment
6. Teacher Education

The six authors are specialists from six European countries who - in the past 20 years - have become known, at least in their own countries, as experts in their field and who, in at least one of the 5 workshops, acted as directors of studies or as animators of one of the working groups.

2. Rationale

The necessity of teaching at least one foreign language to every European citizen is so obvious that there remains hardly any doubt about its justification. The liberating value of stepping outside one's own culture and one's own language has long been recognized in educational philosophy and the competence to communicate in more than one language has become an accepted postulate of modern educational theory. Therefore all national educational systems in Europe provide the opportunity for their citizens to acquire at least a basic communicative competence in languages other than their own.

But should such acquisition of necessity be part of primary education ?

We have to realize that - contrary to the general acceptance of the importance of offering foreign languages to all pupils - no common agreement has yet been reached about the desirability of making it a constituent part of the primary school curriculum. Quite a number of teachers and educationists wish to stick to the traditional practice of starting foreign language teaching at the beginning of secondary education, i.e. at the age of 10 to 11 as a rule.

Therefore our present compendium has to include a rationale for foreign language education at the primary level and must present an overview of the principal arguments for the introduction of foreign languages into the primary school curriculum.

These arguments fall into four categories and stem from four scientific disciplines:

- Developmental psychology
- Neuro-physiology
- Anthropology
- Pedagogy

a) Developmental psychology

From the early days of research in our field the programmes of investigation contained a good deal of psychological argumentation.
Researchers turned to developmental psychology as the discipline directly concerned with the changes in people's dispositions and behaviour, and wanted to learn what this discipline had to offer.
Arnold Gesell was one of the first psychologists who gave an answer to the question of when to introduce foreign language learning into the school curriculum:

> "The young child below the age of 10 enjoys language experience. He is ready to learn, to listen, to communicate by word of mouth, in playful and dramatic situations. With favorable motivation he is emotionally amenable to a second and even a third language." (Gesell 1956)

While Gesell stressed the **emotional** disposition for foreign language learning, Frances Ilg emphasized the **intellectual** readiness of young children. She described these children as, "group-minded, expansive, and receptive. At this age, when expansion and imitation are at their height, the child can under favorable conditions be expected to learn a second language with a rush." (Ilg 1956)

In more recent years Rachel Cohen points to the fact that an early beginning is necessary if a native-speaker-like accent is to be acquired (Cohen, 1991). It is her view that "the younger the better", that the young child is better equipped than an adult, not only because his/her brain is more disposed to language acquisition but also because he/she reads fewer problems into the process than an adult does. Her research indicates that immigrant children of 3-4 years of age, speaking not a word of French on arrival at elementary school, learned French as a second language holistically by involvement in play, singing, repetition, imagination and story-telling. She found that three-year old children very quickly acquired a native speaker accent, that this took longer in seven-year-olds and that 11-year olds, despite much more time and effort, never quite reached the same level of proficiency.

However, there is also considerable opposition to this kind of argumentation from some psychologists who call it "simplistic".

The counter-argument is this:

Human dispositions at a certain age cannot determine by themselves when an ability such as communicative competence in another language is best acquired. They have merely the function of making such an acquisition possible. It is the environment, the educational environment mainly, that is the final decisive factor.

A representative of this more critical position is the Swiss psychologist Hans Aebli (Aebli 1974, p. 182).

b) Neuro-physiology

The second argument is similar to the first, but it stems from another discipline. In their famous book "Speech and Brain Mechanism" (1959) Penfield and Roberts postulate a biological time-table for language learning on the basis of their exploration of the human brain.

They report that in cases of injury, the human brain of individuals below the age of nine usually recovers completely. The implication of this is clear: the early plasticity of the brain is a capital that has to be exploited for second language learning.

"For the purpose of language learning the human brain becomes progressively stiff and rigid after the age of nine ... Before the age of nine (...) a child is a specialist in learning to speak." (Penfield and Roberts, 1959)

Later research has cast a lot of doubt on this thesis. Van Parreren maintains that the physiological argument is weak, because it does not take into consideration the possibility that this early plasticity can be compensated by the more highly developed learning strategies of the older child (van Parreren 1976).

His criticism is supported by a number of empirical studies (e.g. Ekstrand 1979). These authors deny the existence of an "optimum age" for beginning the study of a foreign language.

Larsen-Freeman and Long agree that there are "biological constraints on second language acquisition", but they cannot be interpreted in such a way that as to suggest after the so-called critical period language learning must be ineffective (Larsen-Freeman and Long 1990).

c) Anthropology

The anthropological argument has a better foundation than the two preceding ones. It starts from a principal human characteristic: the individual's openness at birth. This openness enables him/her to acquire a great variety of social, cultural and linguistic norms. For the new-born child anything is possible. However, socialisation normally forces the individual into one particular society, culture and language, and during this process of integration and adaptation the original openness gets lost. Habits are developed, reinforced and consolidated and they restrict the potential indefiniteness. The originally open human being becomes a monocultural, monolingual person.

There are anthropologists who maintain that it is a basic task of all education to keep this restriction within close limits. They argue that this necessary process - a fixation, one might call it - must not go so far as to prevent the individual from experiencing and acknowledging other ways of life, and they believe that foreign language education is a good means to this end. It was a central idea in the work of the German philosopher Wilhelm von Humboldt, who regarded different languages as expressions of different world-views, that if human beings needed the capacity of looking at the world from more than one point of view, then the learning of more than one language was required. In recent years Humboldt's followers have taken up this argument and postulated that foreign language study should be used more consistently as a medium for the reconstitution of a pluralistic world-view.

This claim is implicitly an argument for an early start of FLE, if one takes into consideration that the described fixation is a continuous process and that in all likelihood, one can more successfully avoid its negative effects, the earlier one begins working against them.

11

d) Pedagogy

The above argument surely contains pedagogical aspects, but it is not an educational one *ab ovo*, so to say, - nor are the two others. A fundamentally educational argument must proceed from the situation of European children at the end of this century and it is the task of the school to help them develop the attitudes and competences they need to master this situation. However valid the three preceding arguments might be, the statement that an introduction of foreign language learning into the primary school makes psychological, physiological and anthropological sense is not enough. Such an introduction must be seen to be educationally necessary as well.

A lot has been said and written about this educational necessity and it will therefore suffice to sum up the main ideas and to underpin them with two quotations from prominent educators.

The educational logic is this:

The world has changed. Children meet members of other ethnic and speech communities more and more often and have to be prepared for these encounters. They need what we specialists call intercultural communicative competence fairly early. For this, they must acquire verbal skills in at least one other language and knowledge of other cultures. And if, as psychological and physiological findings tell us, they possess the necessary dispositions for the competence needed, then it is an educational obligation for educators to help them achieve such competence.

To quote one of the great early protagonists of FLE in the primary school, H.H. Stern:

> "The acquisition of a foreign language must become part of the basic literacy of the child on a par with reading and writing. It is argued that the traditional point of view of primary education as vernacular education is unrealistic, because even by a narrow definition of bilingualism at least half of the world´s population is bilingual; and in any case everyone lives in a world in which many different languages are spoken and therefore it is not defensible to create through education a rigidly monolinguistic setting. If education is to reflect the realities with which we have to live, other languages and other cultures should impinge on children from the earliest stage of formal education." (Stern 1969, p. 26)

Finally to cite an outstanding contemporary advocate of primary foreign language education, John Trim, who adds some specification to the general educational argument:

1. "Modern language work can make a contribution to the general education of the young child and can enable him to develop a positive attitude towards other ways of thought and other cultures.

2. A wholly oral approach, which is possible for a longer period at this early stage and which may be less acceptable later, allows more pupils to succeed in modern language work.

12

3. Many language learning activities which are considered necessary for beginners appear childish to the 11- or 12- year-old but are acceptable at 7, 8 or 9 years of age.

4. The introduction of a first foreign language at an early stage may facilitate the introduction of a second foreign language at a later stage in the course."
   (Trim 1995, p. 39)

These four major tenets will be revisited, explored and elaborated in some of the succeeding chapters.

The introduction and implementation of a foreign language in primary education differs from one country to the other. The social, economic and educational background of a country determines to a considerable extent "why" and "how" a foreign language is introduced in primary schools. Each of the contributors describes the European context within which their thinking has developed and links this to the findings of the various workshops mentioned in the introduction.

It is our hope that the discussion which might ensue from the contributions will be of interest to a wide range of audiences: teachers, teacher educators, curriculum developers, course-writers, policy makers and researchers. We also hope that, as the various early foreign language learning initiatives are further developed across Europe, our present compendium will encourage more of the people involved to co-operate in an extended European network.

1. OBJECTIVES AND CONTENTS
Manuel Antonio TOST PLANET - Spain

In the last few years, the teaching and learning of foreign languages in primary schools has increased greatly in scope; it has developed in all senses, primarily in institutional terms but also, of more direct concern to us here, in didactic and methodological terms. For evidence of this, we merely have to take account of the different reforms introduced into education systems throughout Europe, or to read the agendas for colloquia, seminars, workshops and other training meetings dealing with the teaching of languages: what we still most often refer to (quite wrongly) as **early teaching**[1] plays an ever increasing role.

This is obviously an extremely good thing; however, it does not mean that all the questions relating to this aspect of education have finally been answered, far from it, let alone to any degree of satisfaction. As Littlewood recently emphasized, "as we devise more and more techniques for dealing with the problems we encounter, we also discover that language learning is more complex than we had thought. This means that new problem areas emerge for us to try to understand and solve". (Littlewood 1983, p. 90)

Whatever the case may be, it would seem - more so in primary schools than at other levels of education - that the time has come to ask questions, not in relation to the need to lower the age for these forms of teaching or to extend them (a general consensus on these matters was reached after a long and difficult process), but in relation to the validity and confirmation of everything else : the aims, contents, organisation, methodology, assessment, training required to provide them and so on. Indeed, in this chapter we will endeavour to provide an outline of the current state of the initial aspects cited, while bearing in mind that all such issues are closely related and that only the need for clarity justifies dealing with them in close succession.

We will therefore now discuss the aspects relating to the aims and contents of the teaching and learning of foreign languages in primary schools by recapitulating some of the issues raised in the Council of Europe's recent workshops; the background to and

---

[1] **"Early"** is probably not the most appropriate term to describe the teaching of foreign languages in primary schools. On the one hand, this is because we refer more and more often to initiation to foreign language learning from the age of 3 or 4 onwards, which is obviously younger than primary school age; but on the other hand, it is especially because "early" is a relative term. To a certain extent, it means "in advance" in relation to what would be "usual" ("before the due, usual or expected time", according to the *Concise Oxford* dictionary). We consider that "usual" or "normal", in relation to learning foreign languages in the school context, should refer to those under the age of 8 or 9, or at least no older than that, and become **customary** within our education systems.

a brief survey of the issues relating to the parameters to be considered when defining the aims and contents of the teaching of foreign languages in primary schools; the aims and objectives of such teaching; its specific nature in relation to secondary schools, for example, and a few specific proposals on the aims and contents at this level, relating in particular to social, cultural and educational aspects.

That said however, I must refer, albeit briefly, to the leading role played by the Council of Europe in this field.

1.1 Background and brief survey

In this area, as in others relating to the teaching of languages, the Council of Europe sensed, at a very early stage, the importance to be attached to the "early" teaching of foreign languages, since from the nineteen seventies onwards, it promoted meetings of experts[1] with a view to updating the priority issues relating to this problem. Since that time, the Council has devoted five new style workshops to it (4A, 4B, 8A, 8B and 17), the contents of which are summarised in this publication.

The questions raised by the different specialists, trainers and practitioners during the meetings, in relation to the general scheme of aims and contents, were especially varied and also covered a very broad range of issues from the aims of teaching modern languages in primary schools to their current and future status, via their various functions. We will merely list them, without claiming in any way that the list is exhaustive. Prior to that however, it may be useful to reiterate some of the basic facts which determine such aims and contents.

Referring to the "fundamental questions posed by all forms of modern-language teaching at primary school level", at Workshop 8A Hans-Eberhard Piepho put forward a series of such questions in the form of binary groupings which may be brought together and reformulated under two distinct headings. Furthermore, such questions are a good introduction to our attempted synthesis.

---

[1] Here is the bibliography quoted on this subject by Charmian O'Neil in his work *Les enfants et l'enseignement des langues étrangères*, Crédif-Hatier/Didier (1993), coll. LAL:
• Council of Europe (1973) : *The Early Teaching of a Modern Language*, CCC/EGT (74) 10;
• Council of Europe (1974) : *Report of the Symposium on the Early Teaching of a Modern Language*, Wiesbaden, Federal Republic of Germany, 11-17 November 1973, Committee for General and Technical Education, CCC/EGT (74) 10;
• Council of Europe (1976) : *Early Modern Language Teaching and the problem of continuity between primary and secondary levels*, GIRARD.D, DECS/EGT (76) 24;
• Council of Europe (1976) : *Societal support for the early teaching of modern languages. The effects of public opinion on the motivation and attitudes of children, parents, teachers and administrators*, FOLDBERG.E and SORENSEN.G, DECS/EGT (76) 38;
• Council of Europe (1977) : *Modern Languages in Primary School Teaching*, Copenhagen, 20-25 September 1976, Council for Cultural Co-operation, Strasbourg, CCC/EGT (76) 38F.

What is (or should be) the **status** of modern languages in primary schools?

Depending on the approach adopted to the question, opinions are centred on two different spheres which also contain various combinations:

Integration	vs	**Separate Subject**
Part of the Core Curriculum	vs	**Optional Activity**
Systematic Course	vs	**Occasional Teaching**

Responses to the first of these dichotomies were implicitly provided when it was stated that primary education is or should be essentially pupil-centred, in the sense that teaching objectives and syllabuses must be designed so as to meet the tastes and needs of learners at this level of education. If teaching is to be focused on children, it is necessary to take into account, on a permanent basis, the intellectual, emotional and social development of each pupil, within classroom planning and within the education system as a whole.

On the basis of this observation, it seems easier to respond to the other alternatives in the table, even if of course it means taking into account the particular situations in which several languages are taught and where it is necessary to adapt programmes (we are referring in particular to bilingual regions with correspondingly **full** linguistic programmes).

There remains an initial series of questions which must by their very nature be taken into account when defining the aims and contents of modern languages teaching in primary schools.

As for the **functions** which modern languages are supposed to fulfil at this level, there follows a table containing certain options which are also feasible.

Language Learning	vs	**Linguistic and Cultural Awareness**
Communicative Competence	vs	**Sensitisation**
Primary Education	vs	**Pre-Secondary Education**

There are sufficient possibilities for choices to be made in accordance with the personal "coherence" on which individual teachers intend to base their selection. A certain logic can undoubtedly be discerned from a perception of the functions of modern languages in primary schools expressed by the following demanding sequence: (a) the modern language learning must consist of a proper course of study; (b) such learning must be systematic, and (c) must serve as the foundation for secondary education. This sequence can be contrasted with another one which is equally possible (but less rigid) which would make such teaching an awareness-raising discipline and would constitute a fully-fledged form of primary school teaching[1]. In fact, these options do not appear to have been chosen. As will be seen later, it is rather a sort of middle way which the specialists seem to prefer.

Numerous references have been made to the issue of "communicative competence vs sensitisation". The aim of "sensitisation" in relation to foreign languages and cultures - according to A.M. Kuperberg for example - evokes the idea of simple contact through activities which are primarily based on games and serve little or no purpose in the sense that only general objectives are assigned to them, such as generating interest, familiarising children with pictures of a foreign country, only hearing language in the form of songs, nursery rhymes and so on. Such objectives are hard to assess, and consequently it is difficult to organise any kind of follow up to the activities. Rather than merely being designed to raise awareness, the teaching of a foreign language at this level of education should be perceived as an introductory process.

Although it is true that an introduction into a foreign language also encompasses "sensitisation", broadly speaking the former is broader than the latter and should be understood as real language learning.

However, this form of teaching cannot and should not be perceived as being modelled on the anticipation of modern-language teaching at secondary school level. Thus, for many teachers the response to the question posed would be that the "sensitisation activity" is an insufficient aim for primary schools; at that level, real foreign-language learning should be envisaged, which does not mean however that it should be perceived on the basis of the criteria used for secondary schools.

To come back to another of the alternatives observed (linked to what we have just described), the mediate and instrumental nature of the learning of modern languages in primary schools may not only correspond to a pre-secondary perception of such teaching, but may also manifest itself, perhaps even more than elsewhere, in certain aims assigned to it by some people, be they parents, decision makers, course designers or certain teachers themselves. Thus, Ana Vivet summed up this way of looking at modern-languages teaching (the inherent paradox in which is not always immediately apparent), by explaining that, in many people's minds, there is of course the idea that "nowadays all children should learn a foreign language", but this is especially true because "it will be beneficial to them when they are adults"; the widely-held view is that the learning must start at as early an age as possible, but only because young children have a great capacity for learning languages, and finally that, while it is of course necessary for them to learn foreign languages, these must be the most common or the "most useful" since these are the ones which will provide the greatest benefit in the future. Consequently, foreign languages, even when they are taught from the earliest

---

[1]   **Primary and not "elementary"** in the sense which an eighteenth century educationalist delighted in applying to the term in a didactic work : "With regard to sciences and education, **elements** are to be understood as the **essential components** of a science which, because they are the essential components, prepare us first of all for study and then lead us towards complete knowledge of the subject".

18

possible age, are never designed to benefit or to be of interest to the people learning them, but only become so later, when as adults those people need them. Ana Vivet ends by stressing that "the actual needs of children themselves are ignored and no one bothers to ask what meaning languages can have in a child's life. What does it mean to children of 4, 7 or 10 years of age to discover another language? What do children feel when they discover not only another way of speaking and communicating but also another culture with other values and symbols? What do they get out of learning languages and what attitude do they adopt? Can we say that the learning of languages is positive for their development?" These are all fundamental questions on which it is necessary to reflect when determining the aims and contents of primary school teaching.

This is even more relevant in view of another important factor: the age group under consideration.

This variable strongly conditions the definition of aims and contents: on the one hand, this is because there is no exact equivalence between the entire section of the population under consideration at this level of education (our primary school reference group ranges from the ages of 5/6 to 10/11), the age at which a foreign language is introduced (in most cases this only happens at 8 years of age, and often later) and the different stages which usually punctuate primary education, given the psychocognitive and emotional development of the learners. On the other hand, the period for which the modern language is taught varies, depending on whether it is taught from the age of 8 or 10 onwards (ie whether the period of learning is of 2 or 4 years' duration). In such diverse situations, the aims, contents, function and so on which may be assigned to such forms of teaching vary significantly.

The question of age in primary schools is extremely important, given the fact that it determines for the learner, as has often been pointed out[1], "the extent to which practical concepts, derived from action and from its inherent logic, are mastered, and the degree to which abstract conceptual thought is understood; the level of proficiency in their own language; the degree of familiarisation with metalinguistic activity; the extent to which communication behaviour strategies are mastered; the perception of language as a vehicle for knowledge and the rejection of gratuitous language-related activity", and on the other hand "their egocentricity: the basis of their linguistic needs, their tolerance towards what is alien or the absence of psychological inhibitions, their retentive potential and corresponding non-recall potential".

There is hardly any need to stress the importance of the envisaged duration of the language course, since the fact of how early or late it is actually introduced has sufficient impact in itself. This is demonstrated by various remarks made during workshops to the effect that certain objectives only seem feasible as part of a sufficiently long period of teaching, and therefore depend on the time when the foreign language is introduced.

---

[1]   In particular, by Anne-Marie Kuperberg

In short, a number of extremely restrictive factors determine the selection of the aims and contents of the teaching of foreign languages in primary schools; furthermore, such factors are not unrelated to the methodological and didactic strategies used in this form of teaching.

1.2 Aims and objectives of the teaching of foreign languages in primary schools

General agreement seems to have been reached on this particular point: the aim of the **curriculum** at this stage of primary school - as repeated on many occasions during workshops -is not to **teach a foreign language** but to teach how **to communicate in a foreign language**. Moreover, this both implies and explains why the strategy recommended for such teaching is based or, according to widely held opinion, should be based, on communication and more directly oriented towards the acquisition of real communication skills.

It is now quite clear - as repeated on several occasions - that we are dealing with a complex notion. According to the analysis presented by Jan van Ek, in his essay on the aims of learning foreign languages published by the Council of Europe in 1986, and also quoted during workshops, communication skills are made up of partial or subordinated skills.

Of course, linguistic competence is the essential ingredient in the ability to communicate: it represents detailed knowledge of linguistic forms (words, structures and phrases) which are necessary for the performance of linguistic acts in relevant communicative situations. However, such competence is not sufficient. All linguistic acts are performed in a sociocultural context and are therefore governed by a situation which differs between cultures and languages. According to van Ek, this gives rise to the idea that "the use of a particular language implies the use of a reference frame which is at least partly determined by the sociocultural context in which that language is used by native speakers. Competent use of that language, then, presupposes a certain degree of familiarity with that sociocultural context". (van Ek 1986, p.35)

Therefore, sociocultural competence is another basic element of communication, and consequently a fundamental objective for learning a foreign language in the primary school context. However, apart from the linguistic and sociocultural aspects, teaching a modern language at this level also includes objectives which relate both to the effect and the general objectives of elementary level education. Some of them have been defined as essential by the experts participating in workshop 8B, in particular those consisting of :

-   recognising a foreign language as a valuable and desirable means of communication
-   using a foreign language despite limited linguistic abilities
-   enjoying using a foreign language
-   accepting someone or something which is unfamiliar or strange

- practising tolerance and intercultural understanding
- enriching one's personal experience through contact with other cultures

In other words, the overall objective in teaching a foreign language at primary level should be to generate in children an essentially positive attitude towards the language being learnt.

The sense and the functions of teaching and learning foreign languages in primary schools also make a decisive contribution to general educational objectives. Knowledge of a foreign language and the ability to communicate in it both provide a vital form of assistance in achieving proficiency in one's native language. Furthermore, coming into contact with other cultures by means of a foreign language promotes understanding and respect for other ways of thinking and acting, and provides a broader and richer vision of the real world. Knowledge of foreign languages therefore makes a twofold contribution to the ability to communicate and also to pupils' psychocognitive development.

1.3 The objectives assigned to the teaching of foreign languages in primary schools

Having reached this point, we can make a proposal relating to the general objectives to be assigned to primary education, if not as a model then at least as a noteworthy example, which seems however to be a kind of synthesis of the different proposals studied in the various Council of Europe workshops on the issue. In any case, it draws copiously on the current perceptions held by experts in the discipline. Furthermore, the proposal - which we have drawn and adapted from the curriculum project contained in the Reform of Primary School Teaching in Spain - was the subject of various discussions at Workshop 17. To a certain extent, it bases the general objective of the teaching of foreign languages in primary schools around two main spheres: one concerns communication skills directly and the other relates to educational aspects, the components of which (cognitive, emotional, social and intercultural) are obviously essential at this level. Accordingly, the teaching of foreign languages in primary schools must help to develop the following abilities in pupils:

a. to understand simple oral and written texts relating to familiar and customary objects, situations and events which include information of both a general and specific nature conveyed by the texts for practical purposes;

b. to use the foreign language orally to communicate with the teacher and other pupils in normal classroom activities and in interpersonal communicative situations by adopting a respectful attitude towards the contributions made by others;

c. to produce short and simple written texts which obey the elementary rules of the written code, on themes which are familiar to pupils;

21

d. to read, with a view to understanding, short and simple texts related to classroom activities and which take account of the knowledge pupils have of the outside world, as well as their experiences and interests, in order to obtain the desired information, be it of a general or specific nature;

e. to perceive and appreciate the communicative value of foreign languages and the capacity for learning to use them by demonstrating an attitude of understanding and respect towards other languages, those who speak them and their culture;

f. to understand and use the linguistic and non-linguistic conventions employed by those who speak the foreign language as learnt in everyday situations (for greetings, farewells, introductions, congratulations and so on) so as to make communication easier and more fluent;

g. to **use**, while learning the foreign language, **the knowledge and experience acquired** while learning other languages, in particular one's native language, and gradually develop independent learning strategies;

h. to **establish relations** between the sense, pronunciation and graphic representation of words and phrases in the foreign language, and also recognise its sounds, rhythms and intonation patterns;

i. **to use non-linguistic means of expression** (gestures, body language, various sounds, pictures and suchlike) so as to try and understand or make oneself understood in the foreign language.

1.4 Contents assigned to the teaching of foreign languages in primary schools

With regard to contents, an aspect whose complexity is ultimately probably greater than in the case of objectives, be they general or specific, we believe after analysing the workshop reports that further restructuring work needs to be done. In our view this task should include taking account of the various components of the course contents, which relate moreover to all the points dealt with up to now and can be represented in outline as follows:

- **Functional and communicative content**, in accordance with the detailed guidelines already developed in the Council of Europe projects, including:

    - greeting, saying goodbye, introducing (oneself and others);
    - identifying and explaining where you are going / where you are coming from;
    - starting and finishing a conversation, giving and requesting information;
    - spelling, naming, counting and calculating, correcting oneself;
    - accepting, refusing an invitation;
    - comparing, locating in time and space;
    - giving orders and advice;
    - expressing tastes and preferences;
    - expressing one's opinion, agreement and disagreement;
    - speaking of past events, describing and narrating;
    - expressing feelings, reporting questions and so on.

- **Linguistic content** (phonetic, lexical and semantic, syntactic and textual aspects): for comprehension and expression, oral and written work (ie the four skills), taking into account the characteristics of learners at this level and in particular their psychocognitive development. There is no need to emphasise the importance of the linguistic content; this is and always has been the most frequently and most broadly detailed area.

- **Social and intercultural content**, for which we also refer to the work conducted under Council of Europe sponsorship. At Workshop 17 in San Lorenzo del Escorial, Peter Doyé presented a report which was all the more interesting since he adopted, in relation to it, the original perspective of the teacher as an "intercultural education manager". Within this framework we will include what is now conventionally called **the European dimension** of teaching foreign languages, which probably extends beyond this area, but represents one of the vital elements of it.

- **Thematic and situational content** which, at this age level are of essential importance; a short list of what it covers is presented below:

    - School, friends and peers
    - Home and toys
    - Days, work, sport and leisure
    - Food and meals
    - Clothes and different times of day
    - Weather (forecasts) and holidays
    - Animals (pets and others)
    - Stories and fairy tales, imaginary journeys
    - Cartoons, comics and so on

and more general topics such as people's behaviour and habits, traffic, money, customs and traditions, ecology, nature conservation.

- finally, **educational content - last but by no means least!** In fact, given the level of education with which we are dealing, such content should even be given priority, since it encompasses all the other aspects. All the factors which help to develop a pupil's metalinguistic consciousness, or which make it easier for him/her to discover a different culture and to assimilate it - which are by definition and in their own right important elements in linguistic and intercultural areas - are also elements of the general educational content which cannot be omitted. To them should be added all the factors which (in terms of the contents, activities and procedures) are designed to initiate pupils into independent learning; all in all, learning how to learn.

I am quite aware that in this chapter I have merely scratched the surface of the wealth of experience gained from Council of Europe workshops in terms of the aims and contents of teaching modern languages in primary schools. The chapters which follow will give fuller body to this outline. It is none the less true that, if there is one question which (as recommended by a certain classical author) needs to be put back through the mill **twenty times,** it is this question of redefining the aims and contents of teaching modern languages in primary schools. I will therefore most probably have the opportunity to return to this subject.

2. METHODS
Lisbeth YTREBERG - Norway

2.1 Basic theories of how children learn a foreign language

When reading the reports from the Council of Europe's workshops on teaching foreign languages in primary school, one is struck by the fact that there seems to be a unanimously positive attitude to teaching early learners, and a remarkable agreement on the methods of such teaching. A unanimity like that may be somewhat misleading, since the workshops are especially conducive to building up a common enthusiasm among its participants, but in this case the possible disagreements are really few and far between.

The focal point of the theories and beliefs on how early learners learn and should be taught, as expressed in these reports, is the world of the child. The concept "holistic" is a key concept, embracing the children's faculties and emotions, their internalised knowledge of the world, and their attitude to life. It also includes the idea that children, as well as adults, have an urge to make sense out of, and reach a holistic understanding of all the diverse aspects of the world. It is up to the teachers, in this case the foreign language teachers, to help them in that process.

Children of 5 - 6 know a great deal about language. Without consciously realising it, they know how a language can be built up, they know the workings and usefulness of a language, and they know that there is still a lot to be learnt. Pre-school learning is experiential. When the children meet the foreign language in school, it is therefore vital that they are given the opportunity to express and develop this fund of knowledge in ways which are appropriate to their diverse learning styles and their emotional and intellectual needs.

In teaching it is usually easier to find common aims and objectives than to agree on how to put these into actual practice. But following on from the consensus described above, there are some basic tenets on which there is little or no conflict of opinion:

Children have a natural capacity for language acquisition, and an early start will familiarise them with the foreign language in ways which are deemed to be beneficial. Close contact with a language makes the children sensitive to the modes and meanings of that language, and at the same time, if the teaching methods are appropriate, they are capable of acquiring significant competence in the language.

The overall aim of the teaching methods is to work through natural communication in the target language. At all times fluency is more important than accuracy, and interaction between the pupils, and between the pupils and the teacher, should encourage this natural flow. Initially the children will not be able to speak fluently or for any length of time. The sensitive teacher will therefore accept the children's use of their mother tongue (sometimes mixed with the target language) if it is obvious from the context that they understand what is going on, and should praise them generously every time they say something in the foreign language. It must also be accepted that many children have a silent period before they try to speak.

Children have different learning styles and different strategies for learning. Class teachers in primary school will usually know their pupils well. They cannot always analyse every individual's learner strategies, but can ensure that the teaching approaches used are varied and exploit the world of the child and the classroom. Short, frequent sessions, a substantial collection of different types of activities and a willingness on the part of the teacher to be flexible, are essential features of primary foreign language teaching. The activities must give the pupils the opportunity to use all their faculties; to look, listen, touch, move, talk, sing and shout! To the old slogan "learning by doing" we may add "learning by playing".

In a sense every learner knows best how he or she learns. Early learners cannot yet express this knowledge, but they should be encouraged to talk about it in simple terms; how they think they remember best or what they like to do and why. Reflections in their own words help to develop their metalinguistic knowledge and that in its turn creates a better basis for more learning. In this process the teacher may be the initiator, but first and foremost will act as a guide or a "scaffold". We aim at more learner autonomy. A development towards self-awareness and the opportunity on the pupils' part to choose freely from many activities will promote that aim.

All good teaching hinges to a large extent on the attitudes of the teacher. In language teaching and learning, not least with the beginners, the emotional tone of the classroom is all-important. Ideally the teacher's attitude is nurturing, the atmosphere positive, friendly and stress-free. Through a variety of activities the pupils will have the opportunity to demonstrate growth and a measure of success. Errors and mistakes should be treated as proof of stages of learning, and under no circumstance should pupils be punished for making mistakes. If the teacher sets a model of this kind the pupils will see that open-mindedness and tolerance are intrinsic features in learning a new language.

2.2   Selection and organisation of content and language

In most European countries it has been decided by school authorities, with the approval of the teachers themselves, that the primary school class teacher should also be the foreign language teacher to early learners. This is obviously useful, because the class teacher knows the children well and is also in a key position to select the most appropriate content and language, and to plan and organise that selection. A successful foreign language learning programme for beginners is dependent on the total programme and its relationship to all the other areas of the primary curriculum. Foreign language teaching in secondary schools all too often means teaching in splendid isolation; the language seen as a little cultural island on its own in the sea of mother tongue. This is an unfavourable position at all levels, but especially so in the case of the young beginners. The fact that the primary class teacher is supposed to teach these pupils, however, is one of the basic premises for a different approach.

When you learn a language you search for meaning. If we realise this, we must arrange learning situations in which the focus is on meaningful content rather than on accuracy of form, and in which we exploit the children's knowledge of the world, such as it is. How is this to be done in actual practice? In the Council of Europe reports, the idea of "embedding" is crucial; the themes and the methods of foreign language teaching should originate from the primary curriculum and develop in close contact with the ongoing work in other areas of the curriculum. An approach from this angle has several advantages. Firstly, it gives priority to topics the children know something about, either because they have learnt about them at school, or because they are familiar with them from daily life. Secondly, teachers can select topics which are of special interest to or serve the needs of their pupils in particular, and at the same time pay attention to the local environment. And last, but not least, the foreign language appears in a natural context.

However there are disadvantages: By definition the embedding model is linguistically diffuse. It doesn't teach a predefined body of language containing built-in progression of vocabulary, grammar and function - which is what the subject model does. There is a danger that this can lead to a rather fragmented learning of language. In the embedding concept the problem of how the various linguistic elements can be put together in a coherent system of language, is particularly great.

An approach based on themes requires good and systematic planning to succeed, and collaboration and co-operation with colleagues across the curriculum. We must, at all cost, avoid giving the impression that activities are collected that pass the time, but have no underlying organisation. The practical organisation of "embedding" will be in the form of daily classroom interaction, but also often in project work or other types of cross-curricular teaching. It is also in the nature of theme-teaching that very few themes can be taught exhaustively at one stage. "Pets" can be followed another year by "Farm animals" and later "Wild animals", so that work on one theme exploits the pupils' knowledge acquired earlier, in a cyclical process. Thus repetition becomes less mechanical, and remedial teaching finds its place in a context which may be less stressful than it ordinarily is. In addition to this, the fact that a theme can be used on any level, will make it easier for the teacher to consider what may work best in that particular situation, with that particular class.

In a system like this, teaching grammar as such has little or no place at the beginner stage. The teacher's main concern when it comes to the choice of language will be to simplify the syntax and to use a vocabulary which is easy without being unnatural. Activities which focus on a certain language point may of course be used, when followed up properly in context, but grammatical terms and teaching grammar as grammar is a waste of time. Very young children are perfectly able to absorb the target language through play and other activities which they find useful and enjoyable. At later stages, however, more systematic work may be useful, but only in so far as it clarifies

27

and makes understandable language which the pupils have experienced in oral production.

One of the objectives presented in the the Council of Europe"s work on foreign language education is to promote cultural understanding and awareness, and it is generally agreed that an early start will give this aspect a bonus. Young children are usually open-minded and curious, and, because they have little experience, they have fewer mental barriers to novel phenomena and novel ideas. It may appear, perhaps, as if the stress on the primordial role of the class teacher and the primary curriculum goes contrary to the idea of the inter-cultural learner. In the possible conflict between "sameness" and "otherness" what do we choose? The general feeling seems to be that one wants both to have one's cake and to eat it. Children who are allowed to talk about their little world and who meet an appreciative audience, will feel accepted and safe enough to explore and celebrate a larger and more foreign world. So, in the selection of themes the personal and local experiences will be the foundation, and the foreign cultural elements the superstructure.

One of the consequences of a theme-based approach is the demand for authentic materials. Since materials with be dealt with elsewhere in this compendium, suffice it to say that in the long run "meaning" in an inter-cultural exchange can only be fully realised in authentic representations of a culture, i.e. texts (in a wide sense) which have not been made specifically for language teaching. However, in the stages of learning the pupils undergo, their own incomplete language is also "authentic", and a text may have an authentic ring to it even if it is produced for the classroom by a teacher or a textbook writer. It is no use being dogmatic if the text is motivating and leads to natural communication.

The same applies for the question of whether to use a textbook or not. We may say that all the arguments for embedding, development towards learner autonomy, authenticity etc. lead to the logical conclusion that teachers should make or find their own materials. Otherwise it is difficult to be flexible and child-oriented. So, the ultimate aim is clear. However, the actual situation in many countries justifies a modicum of realism. Teachers who are not properly qualified and who may be pressed for time do not have the professional skill and energy to do the work involved. In such cases the teachers should be encouraged to try and adjust the textbook to the teaching rather than the other way around, for instance by including locally based topics and materials.

2.3 Teaching communicative competence

In many ways "communication" is the password in the foreign language teaching methodology of today. The stress is no longer on **the** right method, but on a communicative **approach**, which is defined as a set of assumptions on the nature of language teaching and learning, such as the ones discussed above, and which may comprise several methods. For the teacher doing the practical work in the classroom the questions to this will be: How am I to teach listening, speaking, reading and writing? What sort of activities will promote these current basic ideas in methodology?

It is impossible to summarize all the methodological proposals from the reports of the five workshops, but we can at least mention and describe those characteristic features that all the reports present as common traits.

They are

- **Aiming at basic communicative competence**
- **Emphasis on the progressive development of this competence**
- **Visualisation and personalisation**
- **Learning through play**
- **Holistic approach**
- **Oral interaction**
- **Reading and writing**
- **Repetition and frequency of exposure**

2.3.1 Aiming at basic communicative competence

If the overall aim of foreign language education in the primary school is to enable the children to communicate in another language, as Manuel Tost has described in the preceding chapter, then all methodological steps must be directed at the attainment of this aim.

2.3.2 Emphasis on the progressive development of this competence

There is a stress on **training**, on helping the children to achieve competence. Since errors are regarded as part of a natural process, many teachers hold that there is little need to correct and check, especially formal features, whereas positive feedback should be given whenever there is an opportunity. Others say that errors may be corrected, but only up to the point where the confidence of the child is still maintained. Activities should be short, frequent and allow for spontaneous production of all kinds.

The activities should have "high surrender value"; when the children have learnt something they should be able to try it out in interaction straight away and in an ever-increasing variety of contexts. The teacher may use input in the form of techniques which are not in themselves communicative in an introductory phase (a model dialogue, for example). But then imitation should be followed up in meaningful communicative situations, as far as the classroom situation and the participants' imagination allow. If we take a purist's view of the scope for authenticity in the classroom, we must conclude that the only authentic language that can be elicited would be talking about the classroom itself and the situations springing out of being in that room or its immediate surroundings. Every teacher knows, however, that the classroom can be the whole world, even the universe, if we create it together. This "willing suspension of disbelief" is easier to bring about with young learners than with any other age group, and even more important.

2.3.3 Visualisation and personalisation

Any method for teaching young beginners would have to rely heavily on **visualisation** and **personalisation**. Children are dependent on other stimuli than language, and visuals and realia of all kinds are a must. To be experienced and internalised, the target language should be presented so that it is connected to persons, real or imagined. In that respect a teddybear or a hand puppet is as good as a pupil. Children growing up today are also in many ways more sophisticated when it comes to familiarity with visual elements in the media and in daily life than children of a generation ago. As they grow older they may rely to a lesser degree on visuals, but an appeal to all senses will always help pupils to learn. Personalisation also means that the children use the foreign language to talk about themselves and the people around them.

2.3.4 Learning through play

At the beginner stages almost all teaching should have an element of **game**. Playing with the language is very common in first language development and should be so in the target language as well. Through games and game-like activities the pupils are getting motivated and involved. They practise language in meaningful chunks in appropriate situations, learning through all senses. A non-competitive playful atmosphere is the most conducive to learning because a language, even a foreign language, is linked inexorably with a learner's personality. By creating "winners" or "losers" in language activities we gain very little.

2.3.5 Holistic approach

Promoting the four communicative skills is no contradiction to a holistic approach. All the skills are to some extent interwoven and can very rarely be totally separated, and they all involve both social and cognitive processes. On the other hand, to distinguish between them may facilitate an organised presentation, and most language activities have as their **main** focus one of the skills.

2.3.6 Oral interaction

Foreign language teaching is unthinkable without a strong stress on **natural oral interaction**. So, in the first years the young learners spend most of the time listening to and speaking the foreign language, and listening comes first.

Listening is sometimes called a *receptive* skill, but the term is misleading. Most listening requires a readiness and an active co-operation on the part of the listener. It is the skill that children acquire first, especially if they have not yet learnt to read. A characteristic of the listening skill is that once something has been said and listened to, then it disappears and you cannot re-listen to it. This means that the learner will not be able to determine the pace, and will have to concentrate quite hard. Again, repetition and variety in the presentation of input are crucial aspects. The teacher will have to strike a careful balance between overload of language and activities with little meaning. The participatory nature of listening is apparent in many ways, but perhaps particularly so in the case of those children, and there are more of them than we have thought, who need a relatively long listening period before they are prepared to produce anything themselves. When they start participating in productive activities, it becomes clear that they have internalised the previous input just as well as the other pupils have.

A basic activity in all verbal interaction is the **dialogue**. Beginners' teaching uses a lot of dialogue work. The most obvious ones are the dialogues that spring from working in a classroom, like everyday instructions or chat: "Come to the blackboard, please.", "Good work! Well done!" Very often the dialogues will be integrated into stories the children are listening to, and accompanied by movements. Then the pupils show their understanding without having to produce language and they can do it in the safety of numbers. Using fairy-tales is particularly rewarding since the basic story is often familiar to the children and at the same time each country has put its own special mark on it. Perhaps the telling of and listening to stories is just as fundamental in human life as the dialogue. Young children delight in stories, and many beginners' syllabi and textbooks advocate stories as the primary source for content in language teaching.

Learning stories through the ear is invaluable, and so is learning songs, rhymes and riddles. Like authentic stories they present aspects of the cultural heritage, but there are several other advantages in utilising them to the full. First and foremost they give the pupils a feeling for the music of the language; sounds, intonation patterns, rhythm. This is the case whether they are authentic or not. Then they are instrumental in developing metalinguistic awareness. Pupils who play with the language through rhymes and riddles learn to take that small, but important step towards looking at language from the outside which is so useful to the good language learner. And last, but not least, they create a relaxed atmosphere where realism and nonsense go hand in hand.

Since teachers should be careful about expecting too much by way of language production at this stage, quite a few listening activities are made for the classroom and focus on one particular aspect of content and language. They usually expect the pupils to "tick off", "match", "colour", "draw lines" etc. Listening for information in this way is not especially demanding, but even so, the pupils should be prepared in one way or another for what is coming. At the beginner stage the pre-listening phase is probably even more important than the follow-up work expected at later stages of learning.

Speaking is the other side of listening. This is self-evident when it comes to dialogue work and to performing rhymes and riddles and repetitive action stories. Productive speaking is a lot more demanding of the teacher and the pupils. In their own language the children are able to express emotions, communicate intentions and reactions, explore the language and make fun of it. If teachers succeed in creating the right atmosphere for it, this is what they will expect to do in the foreign language as well. Since there are obvious limitations to what they can actually say, the teacher will have to strike a balance between providing language through controlled input and at the same time letting them enjoy natural talk. If the control is too tight, the pupils will soon find the new language unnatural and limiting. Again, the teacher's constant practice in classroom interaction and the teacher's understanding attitude to errors and to accepting the pupils' use of the mother tongue when words fail them, will contribute to free production. After

31

all, for many pupils the classroom is the only place where they can use the target language.

2.3.7   Reading and writing

That listening and speaking are the first and most important skills in teaching beginners, seems to be universally accepted. The role of **reading and writing** is somewhat more controversial. Since many of our pupils at the first stages of school may not yet have broken the reading code, it is necessary to tread carefully. The problem of possible interference between the target language and the mother tongue has not been solved if positive proof one way or another is expected. Experience shows, however, that some types of reading activities can be put to use with success at the beginner stages if they are used with discretion. Primary school teachers who are trained in teaching reading in the mother tongue will have the methodology needed for the foreign language as well.

One of the most favoured reading activities of all, and one which can start quite early, is the teacher reading stories to the children. If the children are arranged around the teacher, or at least so that she can show them pictures and have eye contact with each, the situation itself is both safe and stimulating. When "real books" are used - simple books made for the target language children and with content suitable for the age-group - they have the advantages of being familiar in one respect and at the same time giving access to another culture. Repetitions, talking about the pictures, explanations when necessary and a lot of guessing are all means of introducing the written form of the language as gently as possible. And the best thing with good stories of all kinds is that they can be enjoyed again and again.

When the children start **reading** on their own, it should be introduced gradually and related to their individual development, and the reading should be silent reading. Picture books are excellent starters. The children can extract the essential information through the help of various clues which are not necessarily language-based. If the books have been previously read aloud by the teacher, the reading becomes easier still. And when the pupils have learnt a rhyme or a poem thoroughly by heart, they can look at the text later at their leisure. A teacher-made short text to the pupils' paintings, presented and commented orally in class first, is also a type of text which can combine motivating content with suitable language.

Reading aloud, however, is a separate skill and should be used very sparingly with the beginners; for instance in shadowing the teacher's reading in class or reading labels and short sentences in connection with other activities. Individual reading aloud in class puts a strain both on the performer and the audience which is not advisable at this stage.

In connection with the discussion on when to start reading and **writing** in the foreign language, syllabus planners have considered excluding the latter altogether. Also historically there has been a strong movement towards starting periods of some months up to two years of listening and speaking only. A sceptical attitude to writing is understandable, since the writing skill is by far the most difficult one for the pupils.

Writing very rarely deals with the "here and now"; it is displaced in time and content from the classroom and the pupils' situation, the written code is different from the oral in almost every way, and there is no help from body language and other paralinguistic features. On the other hand, once the pupils have started to read little texts, many of them will expect to write as well. So, when the situation arises naturally, and the children are allowed to take things in their own good time, writing in small measure can even be a good thing. It adds another physical dimension to the learning process. Hands are added to eyes and ears. Writing activities can also help to consolidate learning in the other skill areas. But the most important aspect of writing, and indeed of reading, is that they are means of developing the children's ability to express their thoughts and emotions in the target language.

One of the most useful writing activities at the very beginning is when the teacher acts as scribe to the pupils. The pupils suggest content and words (usually in a mixture of foreign language and mother tongue), and the teacher writes the story correctly on the blackboard. To introduce vocabulary the classroom, the play area or large pictures can be labelled, and the words can be filled into short texts made by the teacher. When the pupils want to write something on their own they should be allowed to use the mother tongue when there are words they do not know, the teacher providing help while they are writing, or later, so that the product is understandable. The main thing is that spelling and grammar are of no importance as long as the activity is motivating and meaningful to the children. Errors at this stage will not fossilise; they show stages in learning.

2.3.8   Repetition and frequency of exposure

Repetition is vital. Short and frequent lessons are considerably more effective than the 45 - 60 minutes lessons of older children. Not only is the pupils' attention span relatively short, so that a short and varied lesson is the most satisfactory. They also forget more easily if the lessons are few and far between. Many of the oral activities used in teaching the beginners are of a repetitive type, and the children love them. There is both safety and enjoyment in participating in something well-known and thoroughly mastered.

2.4   Concluding remarks

As stated at the beginning of this chapter, the consensus on foreign language teaching methodology in Europe is considerable. Many countries start teaching at a very early age, and very likely more will follow. By way of conclusion, however, it may be appropriate to mention some aspects of teaching young learners which have been touched upon, but not conclusively dealt with in the workshops.

The reports show indirectly that there is a lot we do no know about how early learners learn and what the best methods are. More longitudinal language research studies are needed, and development work should be evaluated as objectively as possible. The unanimity in enthusiasm that is apparent in the reports has an element of idealisation of the child which may lead to inflexibility in the face of new and perhaps contrary findings.

One of the most obvious traps to fall into with beginners is a concentration on good **activities** as the be-all and end-all of teaching. Activity can easily be equalled with learning, and unless teachers are firmly rooted in primary methodology, and in valid theories on language teaching and learning, they may fall into just that trap. And in all the communal fun and games and laughter instigated by the teacher there may not be enough room for individualisation in practice, both for the slow learner who needs remedial work and the learner who needs to have more scope for intelligence and resourcefulness. With foreign language as a universal subject and with large classes, more R&D work on differentiation and individualisation is essential.

The workshops have mainly considered traditional ways of teaching and learning. In the future, though, the access to worldwide arenas will open new vistas for communication between classes and pupils. Direct worldwide person to person interaction and document exchange, together with satellite television, will expose the pupils to foreign languages to a degree that we can hardly realise today. Preparing for the effects new technology may have on foreign language learning and teaching is a must in the future.

And yet, despite the changes we may predict or the new challenges we may see, the words of John Trim in his introductory speech to Workshop 8B will surely hold good for a long time, "We promote a communicative approach to language learning and teaching not in the belief that it is the only valid approach to language learning and teaching not in the belief that it is the only valid approach in absolute terms (...), but because we are convinced that effective European co-operation can only be achieved with a great qualitative and quantitative improvement in personal mobility and therefore in the ability of ordinary people in all our member countries to travel for work and pleasure as independent agents. We promote methods which emphasise co-operative interaction among the partners to learning and responsible independence of learners because such democratic practices strengthen the development of a informed critical, independent-minded European citizenry. We support the strengthening of socio-cultural aspects of language learning... because it is only by directly experiencing each other's lives in their national, social and cultural setting, exchanging information, beliefs, values and attitudes face-to-face through a shared language that we shall definitely overcome prejudice and intolerance based on ignorance and fear." (Trim 1995, p. 35)

3. RESOURCES
Rita BALBI - Italy

3.1 Introduction

The teaching of foreign languages in the primary sector has traditionally been associated with an extremely abundant and varied use of resources. Many of them are simple and inexpensive such as every-day-life objects brought into the classroom. Others, such as videos and computers, are sophisticated and require adequate funding. The availability of expensive resources generally depends on national or local policies while a great number of primary teachers seem to share the ability to exploit very simple things to motivate and facilitate learning.

What is a *resource*? Whatever contributes to the learning of a foreign language can be defined as a resource and a good teacher is, of course, the most valuable of resources.

This article however will focus mainly on three kinds of resources: realia, materials, media and technology. For each of the three groups considered there will be a definition and a description of the potentialities and risks involved. The article will also provide some general criteria for the selection and exploitation of resources and present some conclusions and some challenges.

3.2 Realia

Realia means "real things". In the context of language teaching/learning the term refers to real objects used to support language learning. It was first introduced with the direct method and then adopted in combination with various methods and approaches independently from its origin.

Objects of all kinds are traditionally used in many primary classes with the following purposes:

teaching vocabulary

total physical response activities (Example: touch the _____ ; put the _____ near the _____ ; show a _____ ; etc.)

interactive practice (Example: **A:** pass me the _____ please. **B:** here it is. **A:** thank you)

guessing games involving yes/no questions leading to the identification of an object in the hands of a group of pupils but unknown to the rest (Example: is it big? is it made of metal? can we find it in a kitchen? etc.)

practice on the function of identification and description (Example: this is a _____ ; it is a small _____ ; it is made of wood; it is used to _____)

hypothesis making when the objects and their use are unknown to the class or are ambiguous

role plays (Example: buying and selling)

story telling (Example: once upon a time there were a _____ and a _____ that lived in the same cupboard. One day the _____ decided to explore the room where the cupboard was placed and _____)

exposure to some aspects of a specific culture (to the extent the object considered is meaningful in a specific culture).

All these activities may be conducted in other ways and not necessarily using real objects but their use seems to be particularly effective with younger children and in the early stages of language learning. It creates immediate connections between meaning and the language to be learnt especially at the level of individual words and, if adequately exploited, at sentence level too. It may be a powerful aid to memory as it relies on the visual element, on touch, on concrete manipulation.

A special mention among realia is deserved by those "real things" that seem to be particularly attractive for children such as puppets, masks, toys and materials such as *dough, pongo, di-do.*

Puppets can be used to invent characters, for role-plays, to practise all kinds of interactive and descriptive language. Their advantage is that they are real and fictitious at the same time. Ideally they should be made by the children themselves and be the expression of their tastes and choices. The experience of many primary teachers confirms that puppets are good for encouraging shy children to take risks.

Manipulative activities (feasible with dough etc.) and all forms of arts and crafts are an extremely valuable source of language input and creative language use, while at the same time they develop other skills and not just language skills; they are useful in the release of any possible tension occurring when there is too much listening to or speaking the foreign language without any reference to concrete things. Oral work can be very demanding on the pupils especially in the early phases of the learning of a foreign language.

A challenge of the adoption of manual activities during the foreign language lesson is the balance between the language practice and the rest.

Noises and music are a special type of "real things" that can contribute to making a language lesson palatable to the children.

In order to select realia and decide whether to adopt them or not, the following aspects may be considered:

availability: Is the item be readily available or does it require a lot of time and energy on the part of the teacher which is out of proportion to the results in learning? Can the children themselves provide realia for use in class?

suitability: Is the item coherent with the activities in which it will be used and the expected results in learning? Is it appealing and interesting for the children? Has it got potential value to elicit curiosity, creativity, language use? Does the item reflect the culture of any of the places where the target language is spoken? In what way?

exploitation: The potential of realia as a resource for language learning derives from the way they are used and not from the objects per se. Is the exploitation of the item coherent with the learning aim? What impact is it likely to have on the children? Will it be functional to the learning aim or will it act as a distractor?

The dangers to be avoided with the use of realia seem to be:

overuse: It occurs when realia are present in all the activities but are redundant instead of being functional to learning (example: A whole scene of a child sleeping on a mattress and an alarm clock ringing is set up just to teach: "get up, it's seven o'clock").

routine: It occurs when the objects are used in a ritual way and add no interest and no learning to the scenario (Example: A goes to buy a toy. **B** has got the toy that will be requested by A in his/her hands even before the request is formulated) as it happens in the cases when children rehearse their parts by heart in a sort of false role play. Another case of the routinised use of realia is when a very limited number of objects is used in the same way throughout the whole school-year

overcrowding: It occurs when class-rooms are stuffed with all kinds of objects, rarely used and taking a lot of space. The atmosphere resembles a poor quality junk-shop and creates dispersion and distraction.

over-practice of the function of identification and description: This occurs when the language practice is limited to "what is this? It is a _____" and very few other expressions easily practised in connection with realia. The tendency is to extend the vocabulary relative to concrete objects and to ignore other aspects of language and particularly the pragmatic use of language. In this case progression is limited mainly to a specific area of vocabulary and it is immobilized in other areas.

3.3   Materials

3.3.1 Some basic considerations

Materials are the classic resource in most kinds of school learning including language learning.

Materials used in language learning have been traditionally classified as follows:

- course-books

- supplementary materials

- authentic materials

According to this classification the two former groups include materials specifically designed for foreign language learners and generally characterized by simplified language, controlled progression, limited vocabulary. The latter group includes materials designed for native speakers and occasionally also employed for language learning purposes.

A more recent perspective considers texts of any kind just as texts, independently from the fact that they were originally written for native speakers or for language learners. According to this classification the distinction is between course-books (manuals for language learning) and supplementary materials including a variety of texts ranging from labels on tins of food, sentences on T-shirts, to teacher-made lists of questions for a class survey.

In both cases the concept of supplementary material covers more than the concept of text as it includes any material supporting language learning such as pictures, flash-cards, cue cards etc.

3.3.2   Course-books

While at other levels of schooling the adoption of a textbook is often taken for granted this is not always the case in the primary sector. However there are many published courses for children and national and international publishers are taking an increasing interest in this sector. In recent years textbooks for the primary have changed a lot. They are no longer shorter versions of books for older students but tend to integrate the cross-curricular dimension and the language focus.

Course-books generally consist of a Teacher's book, a Pupil's book, a work-book, audiocassettes and, in some cases, video-cassettes. Each of these components has its specific role. The **Teacher's book** provides a rationale for the whole course, suggestions about the introduction and practice of new language items in connection with the pupil's book, advice for class-room management and about how to give instructions in the target language. Some Teacher's books also offer examples of tests and photocopiable additional material for the children.

Some **Teacher's books** are in the target language and some are in the native language. Both solutions have advantages and disadvantages. The former may require more time and effort on the part of the teacher at the beginning but, in the long run, it may result in an improvement of the teacher's language competence deriving from the daily exposure to a text written in the target language. The latter may be easier and quicker to use for teachers with poor command of the target language but might reinforce in them the idea that the native language is to be used when important messages have to be transmitted while the target language is to be considered merely as an object of study. Besides, if a teacher prepares lessons with a Teacher's book in the target language s/he will be more easily tuned with the target language when delivering the lessons.

The **Pupil's book** and the workbook are the main tools in the hands of the learners.

The Pupil's book introduces new language items progressively and provides activities in the four skills or some of them.

The **workbook** provides further practice of the items introduced in the Pupil's book. The activities in the Pupil's book are often designed to be done by the children in an autonomous way.

Cassettes provide materials for listening comprehension and a correct model of speaking. They should be of good technical quality. The debate about the right speed for the speakers is endless: should they use normal speed and be perhaps less comprehensible or should they be slower and more comprehensible? What kind of models are the best for children? Children's voices or adult voices? A standard accent or a variety of accents?

Generally the cassettes accompanying books for the primary also contain a lot of songs, rhymes and stories.

As said above, the adoption of a text-book in the primary is not general and the debate about its supposed advantages and disadvantages is still open.

The reasons <u>against</u> the adoption of a text book seem to be that:

- a textbook is superfluous when the objective of the foreign language is just "sensibilisation";

- a text book is superfluous when the curriculum assigns one hour or one and a half hours per week to the foreign language;

- a textbook may not be coherent with an approach to the Foreign Language relying mainly on project work, integration of the target language with other areas of the curriculum, topic work;

- a text book, to a certain extent, pre-determines the contents of a course while it is better to plan for the course being open to the children's changing interests and their pace of learning.

The reasons <u>in favour of</u> the adoption of a text-book seem to be that:

- a text-book provides a coherent learning plan and correct and adequate language input;

- a text-book is a necessary support for the teachers whose command of the target language is limited;

- it is too time and energy consuming for teachers to design all their materials while it is wise and feasible to integrate the course-book with teacher made and other materials;

- only the teachers who would feel like writing a text-book themselves can do without one;

- a good book can lead teachers to better practice;

- the habit of taking bits and pieces from various textbooks does not lead to much progression in the long run. The goal of the foreign language lesson goes beyond that of entertaining children with activities good and pleasant per se but with no link among each other and no clear learning aims.

For a check-list to analyse course books see Appendix 1.

As a conclusion about this issue I think we should consider both teachers and children. There's no ideal book for all circumstances, but books that work in specific situations. Both the teacher and the children should feel at ease with the book. A teacher should not be forced to work with a course book which is not consonant with his/her personality. Children should find in the course-book a clear and supportive reference point and should be taught to find things in their book.

3.3.3   Supplementary materials

Supplementary materials reinforce, recycle, integrate and expand the contents of the course-book (or basic material when no course-book is adopted).

Supplementary materials have an important role in language learning, as they provide additional opportunities for exposure to the target language and practice, avoiding repetition and boredom.

Some supplementary materials may be used by the teachers to get new ideas for activities or to make lessons more effective. They are the so called "resource books" or "resource packs" with ideas and materials for presentations and activities of various kinds. In this case the teacher has a mediating role and generally adapts the material to his/her needs. In fact, a characteristic of supplementary materials is that they can be used very flexibly and serve various purposes. The same materials may be suitable for focusing specific language items or one or more skills.

Other materials are designed to enable children to experience autonomous work.

Some materials are suitable for generating production in the foreign language, others for offering extensive exposure to the target language, others serve both purposes as they elicit language production as a response to a language input. An example of this latter case is the following activity: children are given the programme of a fair where various events take place at the same time. In groups they have to decide how they are going to spend the day. This activity implies receptive skills to decode the programme and productive skills in order to make the necessary arrangements.

For a list of supplementary materials see Appendix 2.

In order to facilitate the use of supplementary materials, it is indispensable that teachers organize them according to criteria that make them easy to find when necessary. The organizing criteria might be as follows:

- according to language content;
- according to topic;
- according to type of activity;
- according to skills;
- according to the nature of the material;
- according to suitability for certain age groups;

- according to suitability for certain levels of competence.

When a teacher starts to accumulate materials, s/he will be greatly helped by a serious system of classification giving a synthetic and clear picture of the item and including a combination of various pieces of information. Ideally, a teacher should have his/her database to classify materials.

What makes supplementary materials useful in the learning process is the way they are used. Here are some criteria for their effectiveness:

coherence with the learning goals. Supplementary materials should be coherent with the learning goals and should not act as distractors from the syllabus or stated goals. (The temptation of doing "nice" things with no aim may be very strong at times!).

coherence with the educational goals. Supplementary materials should encourage cooperative learning, creativity, autonomy in learning.

suitability for the target group. Supplementary materials should ideally provide a challenge for learners and require some effort on their part but the effort should not be discouraging. They can provide opportunities for differentiated work, as in some activities, different students or groups of students may work with different materials.

3.4 Media and new technology

Media and new technology are becoming more and more part of our daily life. Children are attracted by them and quickly familiarize themselves with their use at least at basic levels.

Media have a high potential for language learning as they rely on various dimensions (auditory dimension and visual dimension, context provided by the scene, lots of cues in proportion to language input etc.). Cassettes have brought native speakers' voices to the classrooms for more than quarter of a century but the impact of video has proved to be even more effective; children get tired and anxious with cassettes they find difficult to understand, while they are attracted by videos even if they are beyond their language level. Media offer a rich scenario including the foreign environment and gestures used in communication.

In addition, media materials can be classified according to the purpose and audience for which they were originally designed and a distinction can be made between cassettes and video tapes produced for language learning and produced for the general public.

Audio and video cassettes, produced for language learning are often intended as support to other materials. There are however some recent experiences in which the video-cassette to be used in class is the main material and other kinds of materials are meant to be integrated with the visual component.

Computers can be useful in general language practice (grammar, vocabulary) and for textual work (receptive and productive). As the situation is often that two or even more children share the same machine, their use, in the best cases, produces cooperation and exchange of ideas. Another advantage is the experience of autonomous work.

These seem to be the positive aspects. However there are some dangers too:

- children are attracted by the computer but may pay no attention to the language contents and do things mechanically;

- the activities may be limited to mechanical drills substantially of the same kind as the traditional ones; this happens when only linguistically and methodologically poor material is available;

- children have few opportunities to interact with other human beings.

A risk with video is that children watch too much of it during the day (taking into account the use of video in many school subjects and at home) and become passive watchers.

A few very lucky schools have satellite television which provides opportunities for frequent exposure to a rich variety of language and cultural aspects.

The direct contact with other speakers of the target language (native speakers or learners) is generally motivating and produces learning beyond the planned syllabus. Traditional correspondence between schools can be integrated or replaced by the use of faxes, internet, telematics and exchange of video-tapes which offer great potential for direct and fast communication between schools, even if the use of some of these is restricted by budget policies and by attitudes considering these instruments to be at the exclusive service of administrative rather than educational purposes.

As a conclusion to this part, it is necessary to say that even sophisticated audio-visual means and technologies produce learning only when used in a way which is conducive to personal involvement, reflection, interaction and with teachers accepting the role of facilitators of learning rather than that of dispensers of knowledge. The quality difference is not made by the use of the O.H.P. versus the traditional chalk board but by the way the teacher uses the available instuments.

3.5   Conclusions

This chapter has analysed various kinds of resources for the teaching of a foreign language with reference to the primary sector, showing their potentialities and some possible risks.

Here are some general recommendations valid for the use of all types of resources.

i.   Children's involvement

Children can profitably contribute to the provision and design of resources. Besides collecting realia and drawing things they can also provide texts. A very enriching experience is the preparation of books combining pictures and texts written by the children, according to given models or freely. The books can then be exchanged among different classes and schools.

Children can also prepare questionnaires for class surveys, and texts for a treasure hunt and other games. Writing things that will be read and used by other children will be motivating and challenging. The use of computers will add an element of precision and real editing to these experiences.

ii.   Extensive use of materials for native speakers

Children can profitably be exposed to materials for native speakers, especially video-tapes and books and be encouraged to get the most out of them by focusing on the contents without worrying too much about the language details. Hopefully, this exposure to the foreign language will become a normal dimension of their daily lives. Paradoxically, the younger the children are, the easier it is to find suitable authentic materials for them, as the gap between the cognitive and the linguistic level is less perceptible in materials for that age.

iii.   Combination of materials with different perspectives

Children who are not native speakers also need explicit teaching. Their language competence and their language learning abilities will develop through the combination of opportunities for explicit teaching and for natural acquisition. An FL can be learnt exploiting some strategies of first language acquisition but in combination with specific support. School children aged 6-11 are different from toddlers learning their native language. Children will learn more if resources integrate both the affective and the cognitive dimensions.

iv.   Adoption of materials providing an element of choice

The choice can be of contents, of form, of activity, of modality etc. Children will feel at ease if they can choose and not just be told all the time what to say or do. In the case of reading materials, choice on the part of the children is a must.

v.   Adoption of relevant materials

There is no reason to ask the children to work with silly things just because their FL competence is still limited. FL activities should be similar to good activities feasible in L1.

vi.   Teacher training

Analysing commercial materials, adapting existing materials, designing materials (even multi-medial) is part of the teacher's expected professional competence. This requires linguistic and methodological skills that can be acquired with proper training

vii.   Attention to culture

It is generally agreed that communicative competence also consists of intercultural competence, and the awareness of and respect for other cultures (and one's own) is one of the primary aims of the FL. Attention should be paid to the explicit and implicit representation of cultures in the resources used, so that stereotyped images and overgeneralization can be avoided.

viii.   Attention to the evolution of media and technologies

Teachers should be trained to cope with the on-going development of media and technologies, accept the effort necessary to up-date their skills, and avoid both total refusal and unconditioned acceptance.

Appendix 1: Check-list for analysis and evaluation of text-books

1. Structure

- Is there a pupil's book and a workbook? Is there a teacher's book? (how many volumes?)
- Is the teacher's book accompanied by supplementary materials?
- Are there any audio-cassettes? video-cassettes?

2. Goals

- What are learners expected to know/to be able to do after working with the course? Consider: "sensibilisation", communicative competence, language awareness, intercultural competence;
- Are the goals coherent with the national/local guidelines and syllabus for the foreign language in the primary?

3. Approach to language

3.1. Theory of language
- structural?
- situational?
- notional/functional?
- communicative approach?
- natural approach?
- integrated approach?

3.2. Language input
- through examples?
- through dialogues?
- through activities?
- other? (specify)
- through different modalities?

3.3. How is new language understood?
- through pictures?
- through translation?
- through concept questions?
- building on known language?
- other?

3.4. How is new language practised?
- through drills?
- through controlled activities?
- through semi-controlled activities?
- through free-practice?
- through communicative activities?
- through cross-curricular activities?

- through a variety of modalities?
- is the practice coherent with the stated goals?
- are there any activities leading to autonomy?

3.5. Treatment of the four skills
- focus on listening- comprehension?
- focus on speaking? (self expression? interaction?)
- focus on reading-comprehension?
- focus on writing? (written exercises? communicative writing? creative writing?)
- focus on the integration of the four skills?
- focus on receptive skills?
- focus on productive skills?

3.6. Language contents
- organized according to a linear sequence?
- organized according to a cyclical sequence?
- no organization is evident?
- focus on vocabulary?
- focus on structure?
- focus on functions?
- focus on notions?
- balance between focus on vocabulary and the rest?
- is there any axplicit teaching of grammar?

4. Approach to culture

- What is the context of the book? (no explicit reference to any place? in a country where the target language is spoken? in the native country?)
- is there any explicit teaching of culture?
- is the approach to culture prescriptive or descriptive?
- is culture introduced through   description?
  "   "   discovery and awareness raising activities?
  "   "   observation?
  "   "   photos?

5. Songs

- easy and pleasant rhythm?
- difficult music?
- easy language?
- difficult language?
- are the songs authentic or written for language learning?

6. Games

- suitable for indoor-activity?
- suitable for out-door activity?
- competitive or cooperative?
- suitable for small groups?
- suitable for the whole class?
- encourage production in the target language?
- do not require production in the target language?
- are instructions clear?

7. Lay-out

- consistent lay-out for each unit?
- clear lay-out?
- pictures? photos?
- if there are pictures and photos, observe their role (help comprehension? just ornamental? support to cultural information? etc.)

8. Cassettes

- do they provide varied and natural models of speaking?
- do they provide materials for listening comprehension?
- do they provide songs?
- do they provide rhymes?
- adequate sound quality?

Appendix 2 : List of supplementary materials

pictures of objects, people, places etc. can be used in ways very similar to the ways realia are used

sets of pictures illustrating a story are suitable for story-telling; listening comprehension; creative work (invention of an alternative conclusion, invention of a conclusion, hypothesis about what happens in the middle showing just the first and last picture etc.)

copies of money of the foreign Country are suitable for role plays (buying and selling), mathematical activities, culture, practice on the notion of quantity

charts with key sentences are suitable as reference for the children to self monitor their production

dictionaries are suitable to teach self help skills

maps of places and countries are suitable to learn about the foreign country (geography and culture), to work on the notion of space, to work on descriptions etc.

miniature models of houses and buildings, generally made of cardboard, are suitable to learn about culture and geography, to construct a model village/town and to work on the notions of space and time, on descriptions, on comparison, on asking and telling the way etc.

simplified readers are suitable for general language reinforcement, to give a sense of achievement as they are generally user friendly; not very appropriate to acquire reading skills as they require extremely limited strategies

cue cards are suitable to stimulate communication and interaction and the use of previously learnt language going against the tendency of many learners to rely on a very limited use of language (Example of a typical routinary exchange: what did you do yesterday evening? I watched TV; with cue cards answers may vary!)

FL found in the native country advertisements, T-shirts, labels, foreign words found in newspapers are suitable for discovery work, awareness of the presence of the foreign language in one's own country, awareness of both cultures, discovery of meaning etc.

authentic materials (comics, books, activity books originally produced for native speakers) are suitable to encourage exposure to the target language in order to start enjoyng and absorbing it in a natural way; also suitable as a challenge and to learn how to cope with partial understanding *board games* provide practice in the four skills in a natural context and interaction opportunities; some games are suitable to learn about culture (differences and similarities)

charts with key sentences provide reference and facilitate self-correction and self-monitoring

train and bus schedules are suitable for general educational aims (probably children are not familiar yet with this type of text), to practise the time etc.

grids, questionnaires are suitable for practising specific language items and to give the children oppportunities to express the content they like.

menus, recipes are suitable for culture and many receptive and productive activities.

4.   ORGANISATION, INTEGRATION AND CONTINUITY
Hanna KOMOROWSKA - Poland

4.1 Basic principles of primary foreign language education

Any discussion of organisation, integration and continuity in primary foreign language education needs a commonly understood frame of reference. The frame of reference we are looking for can be found in projects carried out in several European countries, as part of the new-style workshops of the Council of Europe, which seem to form a solid base for a negotiated set of principles and reasons for language teaching in the European countries.

The crucial statement for our consideration is that everyone should be given the skills to participate in future societies, and therefore, every child should be given a chance to learn a foreign language, not just the gifted ones, although individual differences have to be taken into account (Page 1993:28).

The arguments for the inclusion of a foreign language in the primary school curriculum are often related to future rather than actual needs of the children. It is therefore important to stress the role of language learning as a valuable experience for the child. As Ana Vivet put it in her presentation at Workshop 17 , "Children, of whatever age, are not interested in foreign languages as such...Foreign languages can introduce children to a world of sounds, positive sensations, new discoveries and stimulating acquisitions which go far beyond the narrow boundaries of a monolingual and monocultural education. Considerable benefit is drawn from such experiences long before children become adults." (Vivet 1995:6).

Foreign language learning supports the overall development of the child. As stated at the Council of Europe Workshop 8B at Velm, "foreign language learning enhances the child's ability to communicate, to listen and react. He becomes more self-confident through development of personal and social skills. Through learning a foreign language he gains an awareness of his mother tongue. Furthermore he is able to distinguish different sounds, rhythms and cadences. The child becomes highly motivated to discover the wider world around him. Foreign language learning and teaching can also be understood as fun and laughter therapy." (Hurrell 1995:72).

Even if organisation of primary foreign language education poses problems and if ensuring continuity of this education in both the primary and the secondary sector calls for additional measures, the result is definitely worth the effort. As is explicitly stated in the recommendations of the Council of Europe Velm Workshop, Austria, May 1995 (Felberbauer and Heindler 1995:155), "we consider that it is feasible and desirable for one or more modern languages to be introduced into the primary school curriculum for all children from the age of 8. Policies should be developed leading to the availability of a certain variety of languages. We also recommend that steps be taken to create conditions under which the starting age can be progressively lowered so that an element of modern language experience of an appropriate kind can be present throughout a child's school career. In order to create these conditions appropriate guidelines should be drawn up covering objectives, materials and methods."

The statements above will form a frame of reference for the discussion of organisation, integration and continuity in primary foreign language education to which we now turn.

4.2 Overview of outstanding issues in primary foreign languages education

Although the basic principles and ideas outlined above have received the fullest support from member states from the very start of the project, a number of more specific issues remained to be resolved in the research and development phases.

Questions relating to organisation, integration and continuity, were posed at the Council of Europe Workshops 4A and 8A and were elaborated in the two-year research and development networks, with the aim of exploring these issues. A consensus has been reached in most of the important issues as will be seen in the sections to follow.

4.2.1 Integration and embedding

Integration seems to be the most important factor of all, as it has a bearing on practically every other issue involved and is now generally postulated as the ideal solution and the only way forward in primary foreign language education. This answers one of the most important questions at the start of the R&D action programme of the Council of Europe, that is, whether integration of foreign language teaching with the rest of primary education should be sought or whether languages should be taught as separate subjects. As stated at Workshop 8B, where results of R&D action programmes were presented, more realistic and relevant connections can be made in all aspects of the child's learning whenever integration is introduced and greater opportunities exist to recycle the foreign language in ways and contexts which are consonant with the child's normal learning environment.

Integrating foreign language learning in the primary curriculum will:

- help support the work of the children in all areas of the primary education and especially in the mother tongue, mathematics, environmental studies, art, music and P.E.;
- reinforce the overall conceptual development of a child giving him/her confidence and enhancing his/her motivation (Brewster et al 1992:37);
- help children learn how to learn, by supporting cognitive strategies such as comparing, classifying, predicting, problem-solving and hypothesizing (Brewster et al 1992:37).

As identified by Hurrell, in order to do so, the choice of themes for foreign language learning must be determined by the primary curriculum rather than by a predetermined linear progression in the foreign language. The teacher who delivers the foreign language will seek opportunities to complement and support the child's learning in other areas rather than follow his own foreign language path, thus making natural links with the ongoing work of the class.(Hurrell 1995:74)

Brewster et al (1992:41) give a comprehensive list of the most common areas which can be linked to the foreign language, thereby supporting the development of foreign language learning and consolidating learning in the other areas of the curriculum. We cite some of the examples.

Maths: numbers, counting and quantity, measuring, telling the time.
Science: animals, outer space, how seeds grow.
History: understanding chronology and the passing of time, prehistoric animals.
Geography/Environment: shops and shopping, parks, sports and games, using maps and
          atlases, the weather and climates.
Cultural Studies:the everyday life of ordinary people, festivals around the world, food
          and music from other countries, other cultures and our own.
Art & Craft:drawing and printing, making masks, puppets, clocks, making collages and
          posters.
Music and Drama:songs and rhymes, role play and dramatisation, miming.

The primary curriculum typically stresses the development of literacy and numeracy, understanding concepts connected to mathematics, science and social studies, thinking skills and creativity. Integration is more likely to be successfully implemented, to use Ellis's framework (Ellis 1984), through topic (message) and activity-oriented language learning, rather than by medium-oriented learning.

Enquiry-based and discovery learning centred around particular themes will support the child's overall development and thus help integration.

Recommendations of the Council of Europe nowadays move towards full integration through the medium of embedding the foreign language teaching in aspects of the primary curriculum. This implies, "permeating the daily happenings with the foreign language and the primary curriculum through developing cross-curricular links......Embedding....might include bringing in the pupils from the playground, settling them down, doing the register, organising groups, talking about the date and the weather and managing the class in the foreign language." (Hurrell 1995:73)

Embedding naturally implies operative knowledge of the language, fluency and competence on the part of the teacher as well as a considerable degree of linguistic competence. Recommendations of Workshop 8B in Velm stress the necessity "to ensure the continuing linguistic competence of the primary class teacher" and "the ability to present the foreign language appropriately to children, to paraphrase when the children's understanding breaks down and to amplify for those children who wish to push their knowledge of the language further." (Hurrell 1995: 78-9)

If a class teacher, implementing the idea of integration and embedding, is a competent speaker of a foreign language and a qualified foreign language teacher, implementation is a relatively smooth process.

If this is not the case, intervention of an appropriately trained teacher may be required and this would inevitably lead to the foreign language being taught as a separate subject with its inherent problems. A considerable degree of collaboration between the class teacher and the foreign language teacher would then be needed. Both teachers would be required to engage in joint planning so as to embed the foreign language in daily activities and integrate it with the ongoing work of the class. To facilitate cooperation, it is recommended that an additional hour for meetings be allocated within the regular teaching load of class and foreign language teacher, to determine curricular areas to be supported by the foreign language and to plan learning contexts, topics and activities.

4.3 Organisation and implementation of foreign language education in primary schools.

As follows from the above, it is now widely accepted that the foreign language should permeate the primary curriculum and thus acquire the status of a core element.

This aim, however, can be achieved only in countries where teacher provision is adequate to the needs of primary education. Due to teacher shortages in the educational systems of many new member countries of the Council of Europe, the first foreign language, realistically, can only be placed within the core curriculum at a relatively late stage. Such decisions are pragmatic solutions already adopted in a large number of educational systems on the basis of the assessment of the present teacher provision and should not be considered as an indicator of the current philosophy of education. This, however, means that it does not seem possible to expect an early start in all the primary schools of all the member countries of the Council of Europe in the near future, though the idea should be widely promoted.

The situation, as described above gives rise to the question of equal educational opportunity. If the teacher provision is not adequate, should a delayed start in foreign language learning be equally distributed, or can those children who are lucky enough to attend adequately staffed schools be given the opportunity of an early start? It seems reasonable to forsake uniformity in the short term and permit an earlier start whenever possible and such is indeed the present situation in many member countries.

If contexts of primary foreign language education differ considerably within the national system, curriculum staging should enable some children to benefit from the early language start and at the same time make it possible for other children to join the course at a later stage of education when learners from several lower level schools meet in higher grades. This presupposes slightly different approaches to the development of progressive linguistic competence at various stages of foreign language education in primary schools (5/6 to 10/11).

4.3.1 Early stages of developing progressive linguistic competence in the young learner

The following **broad aims** seem to be important at earlier stages of foreign language learning as identified at the Council of Europe Workshop 4B at Sèvres (Kuperberg 1993:29).

To   develop receptive skills through listening;
       develop a positive attitude towards other languages and cultures;
       sensitize the child to similarities and differences of languages and cultures;
       build motivation to learn more languages.

As far as the child's language development is concerned, the crucial role of the receptive path is fully agreed on here. **Listening** in the primary is of extreme significance as the learning sequence in the mother tongue and in the second or foreign language is largely similar. (Phillips 1993) Children understand more than they can say. Moreover, they understand before they can talk. Providing opportunities for listening is, therefore, crucial. Exploiting all the possibilities here is of great importance due to the fact that listening skills become less active as children grow older and more selective (Kuperberg 1993:29). That is why, especially at earlier stages of learning, the focus should be on listening for comprehension, accompanied by the so-called 'silent period' when children are not pressured into speaking unless they themselves attempt to do so spontaneously. **Speaking** is, therefore, introduced in accordance with the development of the child's motivation to participate actively in the communication process.

Teaching methods and classroom techniques are recommended to cover games, drama techniques, rhymes and poems, songs, role-play, story-telling and practical tasks (Scott and Ytreberg 1990, Argondizzo 1992, Halliwell 1992). Songs and rhymes take a very special place among recommended techniques as they offer pleasure and fun, ear-training, security through rhythm and memory training in forms familiar to and liked by children of various nationalities and backgrounds, thus forming part of the universe of childhood. Stories are also valuable at this stage as they offer opportunities to perceive similarities and differences, to develop the imagination, to train anticipation and to use constant repetition based on structure, which not only forms part of the typical primary practice (Wright 1995), but also contributes to the child's security and well-being. Stories at the same time represent the earliest and most natural form of storing and retrieving language (Gerngross 1995:86).

All the techniques and activities, including those involving speaking skills, aim at **providing input and supporting comprehension through listening** (Krashen 1988). It is often pointed out that comprehension itself should be considered an achievement, "avoiding the widespread practice of evaluating achievement only in terms of the speaking skill" (Balbi 1993:154).

The approaches and methods described above form a condition necessary, but by no means sufficient, to ensure successful language learning at early stages of primary foreign language education. A friendly learning environment is also needed where, as Pollard and Tann put it, every child feels himself or herself a valued member of the class, where the ethos is cooperative rather than competitive and where some children are not marginalized, while others are praised and their work regarded as setting a standard to which other children should aspire. (Pollard and Tann 1990:74) Classrooms which provide a supportive environment of this kind are usually referred to as 'incorporative classrooms.' The psychological role of a friendly learning environment has long been highlighted as supportive not only for school learning in general (Holt 1984a, Holt 1984b, Wolff 1981) but also for language learning in particular (Krashen 1988).

In order to achieve broad aims and implement the methodological approaches appropriate at earlier stages of foreign language learning the teacher should display a considerable degree of linguistic competence and pedagogical ability, as well as:

- 'nurturing skills' enabling the teacher to satisfy the emotional needs of the children as individuals and to unify the class;
- social skills and the ability to communicate with parents and the wider community;
- skills and abilities to cooperate with other staff members;
- a positive attitude to the potential learning ability of all children;
- planning skills and the capacity to reflect on aims and realisable learning outcomes.
(Doyé 1995, Hurrell 1995, Nias et al 1989, Schimek 1995).

The list of skills needed in primary foreign language teaching presented above contradicts a popular belief that primary school teachers do not need a solid preparation. Teaching young learners calls for the profound linguistic, educational, psychological and cultural preparation of the teacher and demands high qualifications including social and communication competences (Doyé 1995a).

Availability of qualified teachers is, however, still far from satisfactory in many of the member countries of the Council of Europe. Due to large numbers of unqualified teachers in the primary education sector, educational systems face the danger of methodologies which are inappropriate for the age group of 5/6 to 10/11. A serious language problem also arises. Unqualified teachers feel obliged to conduct their lessons in a foreign language without having true operative knowledge of it. Recommended methods and techniques should, therefore, favour the use of authentic and adapted listening materials, cassettes, records and videos to compensate for the lack of a natural source of linguistic input. Language problems should obviously be dealt with by in-service teacher training programmes.

4.3.2 Later stages of developing progressive linguistic competence in the young learner

Broad aims of foreign language programmes ought to follow the concepts outlined in the Threshold Level 1990, thus including

- communication ie. the effective use of the foreign language for communicative purposes;
- intercultural understanding ie. respect for and acceptance of other ways of doing things and other beliefs and values which presuppose the appreciation of similarities and differences between their own and other cultures/communities where the target language is spoken;
- self-reliance or responsibility for one's own learning;
- social development, confidence and willingness to attempt to communicate with others;
- the European Dimension ie. the contribution of language learning to preparation for democratic citizenship (Sheils 1993:38).

In foreign language education in primary schools communicative objectives are of great importance and so is their so-called 'washback effect' on mother tongue learning as well as on general communication and conversational skills.

A special emphasis in primary foreign language education is, however, given to intercultural, social and attitudinal objectives, to:

- develop a positive attitude towards other languages and other cultures;
- develop tolerance and acceptance of other cultures;
- broaden the viewpoint of the children;
- share developmental experiences which prepare children for a ready acceptance of people from other countries;
- accept a foreign language as an educational experience for life (Schimek 1995:50-51).

This places a great responsibility on the teachers who should themselves avoid stereotypes, be aware of their own culture and respect other cultures (Doyé 1995a).

The list of broad aims above answers one of the questions posed at the beginning of the R&D action programmes of the Council of Europe Workshops, that is, whether language or a combination of language and 'culture' should be taught, and whether language ought to be taught as a system or perhaps a degree of cultural awareness should also be included. It follows that, to achieve broad aims including tolerance and intercultural understanding as well as to develop positive attitudes and motivation, learning a language with a degree of cultural awareness is the only way forward.

Teaching methods and classroom techniques aiming at the development of basic language skills at later stages of primary foreign language learning have to ensure procedures appropriate to the needs, predispositions and learning styles of the learners.

A set of characteristics of the young learner is, therefore, indispensable when considering classroom methodologies.

The following characteristics of the young learner seem to be perceived by most of the authors writing on the subject to include:

- a curiosity and sense of enquiry
- open-mindedness
- a sense of imitation, love of practice for its own sake
- a sense of the power of body language
- competitiveness
- a pride in his/her own achievements
- a sense of fun
- knowledge of how to exploit an appreciative audience
- the will to transcend adult borders of race and creed

(Fechner 1992:57, Hurrell 1995:71).

As far as language learning is concerned, the following characteristics tend to be most commonly quoted. Children very frequently demonstrate:

- a short concentration span
- a predisposition for kinaesthetic learning modes
- preferences for whole-body learning
- concentration on the here and now
- understanding of the situation, prior to understanding of the foreign language used
- quick learning accompanied by quick forgetting
- the predominance of mechanical over logical memory
- the lack of inhibitions about speaking
- the willingness to make errors and to make errors work for them

(Faw and Belkin 1980, Hardy et al 1990, Wilson 1990).

All the above characteristics of the young learner allow us to draw quite a detailed picture of the most appropriate approaches and methods to adopt in foreign language teaching and learning. These will include:

- holistic, multisensory approaches involving stories, rhymes, songs, rhythm, visualisation and movement is recommended based on the kinaesthetic, visual and audial learning styles of the young learners;
- comprehension based approaches are advocated due to the mostly receptive language learning of the young learners;
- active and playful learning, activity based learning, learning by doing and Total Physical Response are encouraged due to the physical mobility of the children and to their sense of enquiry;
- teaching language in a meaningful context is necessary to support comprehension and to stress the here and now;

- child-centred selection of authentic content meaningful for the children and understandable by them is recommended in order to help receptive learning;
- a syllabus organised around thematic areas is recommended in order to develop and sustain motivation;
- no formal training in grammar is recommended due to the domination of mechanical over logical memory;
- methods strengthening children's memory are recommended due to the dominance of mechanical over logical memory at this age;
- noise and movement should be accepted as part of the language learning due to the prevalence of kinaesthetic learning styles of the children;
- a stress-free atmosphere ought to prevail with implications for error handling and monitoring in order to maintain natural spontaneity and motivation in young learners;
- positive feedback should be given to encourage success and build confidence which is basic for the child's development;
- risk-taking strategies should be encouraged to develop social and strategic competence as children learn by trial and error, learn from mistakes, display natural competitiveness and lack inhibitions about speaking.

(Scott and Ytreberg 1990, Argondizzo 1992, Edelhoff 1992, Halliwell 1992, Gerngross 1995, Hurrell 1995, Heindler and Felberbauer 1995).

Appropriate methodologies can only be successful when foreign language teaching takes place at a time best suited to the pupils with sessions possibly short, bearing in mind the children's limited concentration span. Frequent sessions are recommended due to the fact that recall in young children is deficient. Because they forget quickly revision becomes essential. Frequent sessions also make integration easier (Schimek 1995:51-52).

Evaluation should not determine the children's future school path. Assessment should not be used to eliminate young learners from the language programme or to signal non-promotion to the next stage in the primary school. On the contrary, it should highlight children's achievements. In order to fulfil these requirements, evaluation should not be given in the form of a mark. Descriptive evaluation is recommended as it consists in observing, analysing, describing and reporting. Descriptive evaluation will help identify, acknowledge and celebrate the children's achievements and provide encouragement. It will stress the strong points of the learner rather than highlight his/her failings and provide a positive account of what the learner can do rather than a negative account of what the child cannot do. Evaluation of this kind, which includes positive statements about the linguistic development of each child, should be transmitted to the next stage and to the receiving teacher, in the primary or secondary sector, in order to ensure continuity and progression of the children's foreign language learning. (Gritsch 1995:106, Hurrell 1995:80).

4.4 Continuity in foreign language learning

While discussing foreign language education in the primary, it is important not only to ensure continuity within the primary sector, but also to think forward to secondary education in order to ensure harmonisation of objectives, continuity, coherence and progression between primary and secondary education levels.

Recommendations of Workshop 8B at Velm identify children's rights as:

- the right to a stress-free transition from one system to another;
- the right to the systematic continuity of learning experiences;
- the right to build on achievements.

Smooth transition between the primary and secondary sector is still by no means a reality in many of the member countries. There are numerous reasons for the phenomenon. The most important of those identified at Workshop 8B were:

- that there is generally little contact between the teachers in primary and secondary schools;
- that secondary schools have an impoverished awareness of the learning objectives in the primary sector;
- that teaching styles and approaches which do not take the children's prior learning into account are likely to demotivate pupils;
- that relationships between primary and secondary school staff are often strained.

As multi-level and mixed-ability teaching is likely to take place at later stages, more pair work and team work will be needed alongside better project and task organisation of the teaching and learning processes. A clearer induction in autonomous learning is also recommended. Learners can then choose from a variety of options, have a say in the shaping of objectives and content, as well as develop their own ability to plan, monitor and evaluate their learning (Holec and Huttunen 1990:17).

Proper curriculum staging as well as due attention being given to learner autonomy, safeguards continuity in situations typical to a change of schools at the primary/secondary juncture. It does not, however, safeguard continuity in the case of change of staff or a change of school within the primary sector. The problem is not that of foreign language learning alone. An integrated curriculum typical of primary education is known to reveal considerable cohesion between areas of experience at the cost of continuity. Later stages of education are more likely to be shock-proof in this domain as they are commonly located within a collected subject-based curriculum with less cohesion between areas of experience, but considerable cohesion within each of them (Pollard and Tann, 1992:99).

It is difficult, if not impossible, to ensure continuity when virtually no cooperation exists between primary and secondary school teachers. Smooth transition can be possible only when models for primary and secondary teachers' cooperation have been worked out and information circulated between primary and secondary schools (Schimek 1995:54). Joint pre-service training in didactics and methodologies might also remedy the situation to a considerable degree (Hurrell 1995:80).

Smooth passage can be facilitated by special transition activities such as performances given by primary pupils in the first weeks of their secondary schools to show what they have learned; primary teachers' visits to the secondary school to see their pupils' progress; secondary pupils' visits and participation in primary lessons to enable them to perceive their own progress; common topic projects; primary-secondary pen-pal activities and local festivals of languages (Gritsch 1995:110).

However, all the above recommendations can only be accommodated by national systems with a satisfactory degree of educational continuity in general. Often enough secondary education becomes a meeting point for both newcomers with no language background and for those with 4 to 6 years of foreign language education.

Taking cognisance of a great variety of classroom configurations in the secondary sector (mixed-ability, broad banding, setting, streaming), it might be advisable in such cases to introduce setting as a procedure enabling learners to be grouped according to their skills in a foreign language rather than according to their age and grade.

Appropriate placement may be helped by portfolios of pupils' work which will show the secondary teacher the scope of the child's experience through creative work, posters, workbooks, reading record, songs, rhymes and some forms of recording of the child's achievement level through descriptive evaluation (Gritsch 1995:110). This will ensure a stress-free transition from one system to another, the systematic continuity of learning experiences and building on achievements (Gritsch 1995:112), though considerable amounts of multilevel and mixed-ability teaching will still enter the picture.

To facilitate continuity, joint cross-sector in-service training and dissemination of good practice should also be encouraged (Gritsch 1995:110-111). In-service opportunities should be created to encourage primary and secondary teachers to share methodologies, insights, materials and successful activities (Hurrell 1995:80). Staff development programmes to include experience in the other sector through team teaching, observation, class swapping are also recommended along with transfer of information through leaflets and headteachers' meetings as well as teachers' networks aiming at joint planning and at dissemination of good practice (Gritsch 1995:111)

All the above recommendations are related to six issues which are considered indispensable to ensure continuity:

  awareness-raising
  collaboration
  transfer of information
  transition activities
  dissemination
  training

4.5 Integration and continuity vis-a-vis multilingual and multicultural competence of the young learner

Secondary education in some of the European school systems makes it obligatory for the learners to take two or more foreign languages. The trend to learn more than one foreign language is definitely growing in Europe and so is the range of languages offered in the European educational systems, a tendency identified at Workshop 8B (Heindler and Felberbauer 1995:45).

According to the set of principles laid out by the Council of Europe in the Common European Framework for Language Learning and Teaching (CC-LANG 94-27, Strasbourg, November 1994) when several languages are taught within the same educational stage, similarity of objectives and methods should not necessarily be sought.

As the Council of Europe states, "curricula should be in line with the overall objectives of promoting linguistic diversity", though at the same time, "it is not necessary for the objectives or kinds of progression in each of the chosen languages to be the same, if, for example, the educational system allowed pupils to begin learning two languages at a pre-determined stage the starting point need not always be preparation for practical exchanges satisfying the same communicative needs" (Common European Framework 1994:75).

Multilingual and multicultural competence at every stage, therefore, tends to be unbalanced due to:

- a greater mastery of one language compared to the others;
- a different profile of one language compared to the others, for example, when the first foreign language learning concentrates on listening and speaking and the second foreign language learning on reading and writing;
- a multilingual profile different from the multicultural profile, for example, a good knowledge of the culture of a community but a poor knowledge of its language or vice versa (op.cit:77).

This should be considered in the process of syllabus design for particular languages as often wrong decisions can be taken in an unnecessary pursuit of the system's uniformity.

Multilingual and multicultural competence then entails diversity of aims, objectives and methods employed in language education offered by those primary schools which introduce more than one foreign language into the curriculum. It also entails diversity in secondary education where continuity of one foreign language accompanies a start for the learning of a second foreign language.

In conclusion, the right to foreign language education implies coherent organisation and implementation of an appropriate teaching programme and a smooth transition from primary to secondary, facilitated by the exchange of information and a sharing of good practice. We should keep in mind the child's right to error and sensitive error-handling and the right to a friendly and supportive language learning environment.

5. EVALUATION AND ASSESSMENT
Peter EDELENBOS - Netherlands

5.1 Evaluation and assessment

In FLE and in the general sphere of education, the terms 'evaluation' and 'assessment' do not have generally agreed-upon meanings. In the context of this chapter, evaluation is considered as the appraisal of teaching processes, programmes, curricula, or institutions while assessment refers to the appraisal of, for example, learning results of individuals (Madaus & Kellaghan, 1992). The title 'Evaluation and Assessment' has been chosen deliberately. Focusing exclusively on programme evaluation or evaluations of curricula or teaching processes would exclude a wide range of studies from, for example, Sweden (Balke, 1990), the Netherlands (Vinjé, 1993) or Hungary (Radnai, 1994). These studies are in fact evaluations, because they appraise the attained level of command in the foreign language at the end of primary schools. By including evaluation and assessment optimally useful evidence can be gathered, analyzed and appraised with respect to FLE in a more coherent framework.

5.2 Evaluation and assessment in the context of the workshops

During Workshop 4A (Report on Workshop 4A, p. 71 ff) assessment and evaluation were introduced by discussing the Scottish perspective on these subjects. Specific topics were: the research aims, the data-gathering procedures, variability and the possible questions for discussion at the workshop. One of the results of the workshop relating to evaluation was that a Network for Information on Curriculum and Evaluation was set up. The aims for this Network were:

i. as far as possible to reach consensus on general principles/guidelines governing syllabus and evaluation, but also, where necessary, to highlight issues that are not consensual and that require further exploration;

ii. to produce a report for Workshop 4B, designed to provide relevant information on what a network has achieved and to simulate/illuminate discussion at the workshop.

In Workshops 8A and 8B the following themes were addressed: a survey of approaches, intercultural learning, curriculum, continuity, methodology, materials and teacher education. Evaluation and assessment were not addressed as separate topics, but were treated as aspects of the work of the workgroups. However, during show and tell sessions, specific information was presented on assessments (Report on Workshop 8A, Vinjé p. 102-106). In the light of this, the following texts will focus on the work of the Network for Information on Curriculum and Evaluation. But none of this work can be appraised without describing the context for evaluation and assessment in several countries in Europe.

5.3 Contexts for evaluation and assessment: differences and similarities

The social and political context in which initiatives have been taken for introducing a foreign language in primary schools is almost unique for every European country. Primary-school children in Holland receive much more exposure to a foreign language out-of-school than do their counterparts in (say) Spain or Ireland. In countries that were formerly behind the Iron Curtain very different roles have been perceived for German, Russian and English as foreign languages. Factors such as these, operating in the social context, must have direct consequences for children's motivation to learn and use the language and the rate at which they make progress in acquiring it (Edelenbos & Johnstone, 1996).

The aims and approaches that underlie developments towards FLE in primary schools also differ dramatically. In Germany for example, cultural learning is thought to be almost self-evidently integral. In Scotland, the political will that was vital in enabling the national pilots to take place initially saw the justification for FLE more explicitly in instrumental terms of business competitiveness within the Single Market rather than as an educational, cultural or linguistic contribution to children's personal development.

Despite the differences a number of common strands may also be detected. First, the emergence of a strong role for national or federal state ministries in validating and promoting FLE within their particular countries. Whereas many of the experiments in FLE that were undertaken some twenty or more years ago were a reflection of the initiatives of interested groups, e.g. of universities, local authorities or schools, the developments currently taking place in Europe generally have a more formal national imprimatur, one that is further encouraged by powerful and influential supra-national structures such as the Council of Europe and the EC (especially through its LINGUA programme). This strong emergent role for ministries has had different sorts of implications in different countries. In Germany, for example, FLE is now seen as an expression of political will and considered validated. In Sweden and Holland, however, the debate on the motives for introducing FLE was carried out at a national level. Evaluations in the Netherlands (Edelenbos, 1993; Vinjé, 1993) and in Sweden (Balke, 1990) were aimed at providing information about the success of the initiatives. It is very much to the credit of the various national or other authorities that they have acknowledged the importance of a research-based dimension to the national programme for their country and provided the funds for this. However, research-based evaluations of this sort inevitably entail tensions and difficulties.

A second aspect that occurs in several different countries is the enormity of the problem of actually implementing a policy for FLE across all primary schools. Even in countries where the social context for FLE at primary school is comparatively more favourable, many years of gradual development were necessary before the foreign language became an obligatory subject and national core goals were implemented. It will therefore take a considerable amount of time before most countries in Europe have reached the point at which they could claim they are implementing anything like their preferred model of FLE, based on an adequate supply of teachers who have been appropriately trained for the purpose.

Any findings from evaluations will have to be examined with careful attention to the context for the development, given that this context may in many cases be one of gradual progress towards a distant goal, with many problems and pitfalls on the way.

5.4 The transition phase

During the periods between the initial A-workshops and the B-workshops, major evaluation and assessment projects throughout Europe were conducted. The outcomes of these studies were monitored by the members of the Network for Information on Curriculum and Evaluation initiated in Workshop 4A (Edinburgh). In the context of this article, a selection has had to be made from the overwhelming amount of publications. For this selection two criteria have been used. First, four countries from different parts of Europe have been included, namely Sweden (Northern Europe), the Netherlands (Western Europe), Scotland (Great Britain) and Hungary (Eastern Europe). These four countries are not representative of the total number of studies published, but offer an indication of the work under survey. Further information about evaluation and assessment projects into FLE in Germany is presented by Bludau (1993), Doyé (1993) and Kubanek-German (1996), in Italy by Taeschner (1990) and Titone (1993) and in Finland by Huttunen & Kukkonen (1995). Second, only the major publications i.e. final reports and articles in acclaimed journals on evaluation and assessment have been used.

Sweden
The Swedish evaluation of the teaching of English in compulsory schools was conducted by Balke (1990). The point of departure for the National Evaluation Programme is the present curriculum (which dates from 1980). The aim of the evaluation is to get a view, as comprehensive as possible, of the school system. Included in the programme is a recurrent assessment of pupils' knowledge, skills and attitudes. According to Balke, all participating teachers find the emphasis in the present curriculum on communicative competence justified. The discrepancy between the actual teaching on the one hand and teaching based on the goals stated in the curriculum on the other hand can, at least to a certain degree, be explained by the inadequate competence of many teachers. The more uncertain the teachers are of their own competence, the more traditional their teaching is and the more dependent on textbooks they are.

The pupils are often exposed to English outside school. A great majority listen to English on TV and to English songs almost every day. Other rather frequent activities include listening to English radio programmes and playing computer and role games. Pupils' answers to questions about the activities in school show that pupils would like more opportunities to speak English during lessons.

Generally, pupils have positive attitudes towards the use of English and are also rather confident in their use of English in real settings, though most of them state that they are able to say only a few words. A majority of the pupils think that it is fun to learn English in school and to speak English during the lessons, but compared to the attitudes towards English outside school, the enthusiasm about English as a school subject is lower. Regarding the results on the achievement tests, it is found that ninety per cent of the pupils attain a basic level of proficiency in each of the four skills. A majority of the 10 per cent who fail in one skill also fail in the others. In tests for productive skills pupils can better show their full communicative abilities. A salient result is the great variation between classes, both in test results and in the self-assessments of school performance.

The Netherlands
Vinjé (1993) of the (Dutch) National Institute for Educational Measurement presented the outcomes of the National Assessment Programme (in Dutch abbreviated to PPON) for English at the end of primary education. The aim of the assessment was to survey, as objectively as one can, results in several fields of education and to describe them as clearly as possible. The final PPON report on English showed that the reading achievements of the average pupil are moderate. On average, pupils at the end of primary school (age 11) can understand spoken English. An average pupil can cope quite well in many simple communicative situations. Vocabulary needed to talk about themes like 'transport', 'the weather' and 'describing buildings' has been mastered most effectively. The words that are most difficult for Dutch children are those needed to describe family relations, time specifications and people's clothing. According to experts, teachers in primary and in secondary education generally consider the mastery level of English to be satisfactory, especially with regard to listening performance. The strikingly good results for listening raise the suggestion that pupils learn English outside of school as well. More than 50% of the children say that they learn the same amount of English outside school. A remarkable finding is that concerning the interaction of two different skills: investing a lot of time in teaching English, using a course with special attention to grammar (as is done in a small numbers of schools) leads to negative performance levels for reading.

Edelenbos (1993) investigated the continuity between primary and secondary education. The results of this evaluation can verify the ideas of the workgroups on continuity in the Workshops 8A (Report on Workshop 8A, p. 67-73) and 8B (Report on Workshop 8B, p. 101-112). According to members of the workgroup in Velm, the reasons for many teachers at the secondary level to start from scratch were the following: 1) generally there is little contact between teachers in primary and secondary schools; 2) an information deficit at the secondary level about primary objectives; 3) different teaching styles and approaches which are likely to discourage pupils and 4) strained relationships between primary and secondary school staff. The evaluation in the Netherlands showed empirically that the continuation problem is mainly perceived as discontinuity in the approach and organization of the foreign language in two subsequent types of schools caused by a lack of communication between the two consecutive school systems (at both teacher and management levels), a lack of didactical continuation and a lack of continuity in subject matter, inadequate testing of pupils at the beginning of the secondary level and the use of information on the level of command by secondary teachers. Although the problem of continuity in foreign language teaching is severe, it is no worse or better than subjects like Dutch or mathematics. The continuity problem will present itself in different shapes throughout Europe, but this study confirmed that the continuity problem in essence is made up of five elements: a communication gap, lack of fine-tuning in aims and goals (at several intermediate stages), differences in didactical approaches and the subject matter offered to pupils, reluctance at the secondary level to acknowledge the learning results at the primary level and shortcomings in initial and in-service training to address the above-mentioned problems.

Scotland

In Scotland evaluations of national pilot projects were conducted by Low et al (1993) and Low et al (1995). The prescribed aims by the Scottish Office Education Department of the first evaluation were:

1. assessment of the linguistic attainments of children involved in the pilot projects, including comparison with those not involved and

2. evaluation of the project courses, including description of and commentary on factors such as the nature of the courses and pedagogical methods which enhance or inhibit the linguistic performance of the children involved.

In this study a number of principles to guide the research approach were elaborated. A range of data-gathering procedures were adopted, drawing on classroom activities and special assessments. Paired interviews were selected as the main assessment method for comparing project pupils (who began their foreign language learning at primary school) with non-project pupils (who began at secondary). Procedures and criteria were developed for selecting pairs, for implementing and validating the task and for analysing pupil performance.

The 1991 paired interviews produced evidence suggestive of an advantage for Project over Non-Project pairs across the ability range. The advantage showed up most clearly in pronunciation and intonation, structural complexity, ability to sustain patterns of initiation and response, use of discourse techniques, communication strategies and readiness to answer in class (Low et al, 1993).

The 1992 paired interviews represented the researchers' first attempt at gauging the extent to which progression had taken place within the Project cohorts from Primary7 to Secondary1 to Secondary2. Essentially the same interview format and coding system were applied again in 1993 and 1994, with increasing emphasis on within-Project rather than on Project versus Non-Project comparisons.

The 1995 report indicates that the great majority of pupil pairs within the Project groups (whether girls or boys, and whether categorised by their teacher as high, middle or low achievers) were able to sustain an interaction with a researcher, conducted almost exclusively in their foreign language. Of the sub-components of communicative competence, there was clearest evidence of grammatical-lexical and strategic competence. The 1995 report confirmed progression within Project cohorts from Primary6 to Primary7 to Secondary1 to Secondary2, in the sense that each older cohort was able to put more language into the same type of paired interview task, though the progression from Secondary1 to the end of Secondary2 seemed less strong than for the other years. Moreover, the research team's investigation of the performance of the first cohort of Project pupils to take the national examinations towards the end of their fourth year of secondary suggested a continuing advantage over Non-project groups: '... the advantage in terms of certificate awards was essentially one of a larger proportion of the cohort being entered for a foreign language, and the results illustrating that this larger entry had been at no cost to the school's performance in comparison with previous years with more selected groups of pupils' (Low et al, 1995).

The pilot phase came to its end in 1995 to be succeeded by a generalisation phase intended to ensure that a foreign language would be taught in all Scottish primary schools. So far as the teaching is concerned there has been a major change of direction, in that it is to be undertaken largely by primary school classteachers rather than by visiting teachers from secondary. A national training programme has been devised in order to equip primary class teachers with the necessary foreign-language knowledge and skills.

Hungary
The main characteristics of evaluation projects in Hungary are that a) they are part of a general framework of educational research at the primary level, b) they treat foreign language education as an organic component of the overall scheme of language and communication development (closely linked with the teaching/learning of the mother-tongue), and c) they all deal with very young learners. This also holds for the projects in which the language component is wholly or partially independent from other research lines. The topics covered in the projects mentioned in this section ranged from curriculum design through acquisition orders to a negotiated syllabus.

The findings to be discussed here have been attained in four large-scale projects that were carried out between 1981 and 1991, some of which have been followed through to the present time. The four projects have similar but not identical backgrounds: projects 1 and 2 embrace the whole of the primary school curriculum, with the language component forming a significant part, while projects 3 and 4 are focused on the language component. The design of the language component in the various projects has fortunately been fairly uniform due to the fact that the researchers happened to be the same people. This meant that the experiences gained in any one project could be directly applied in the others.

The most important findings concern the time factor (Radnai, 1990). The highest correlation between results and time factors can be found in the case of actual classroom hours spent learning the language. The frequency of the lessons appears to play a role in the sense that 5 weekly lessons of 25 minutes are more efficient than 3 lessons of 45 minutes. However, this is only the case before reading and writing are introduced. Later on the effect of frequency disappears.

As to the age factor, older children (age 11-12) have slightly better results than younger ones (age 8-9) in tasks on the word and sentence level. Also related to the age factor is the finding that the ability to perform certain tasks, such as carrying out instructions or simple reading tasks develops rather early. Scores on these tasks do not improve significantly with more exposure or with an increase in age. Results, moreover, show that the complex skill of oral text production behaves in a different way than all other skills. Apparently the development of structural skills depends much more on time factors than does the development of communicative abilities. The acquisition of grammar and vocabulary are not so separable in the case of young learners as they are with older children or adults. A large number of structural items (patterns) are first acquired as 'chunks' in the form of vocabulary units. The processes of analysis and synthesis, however, do appear very early in children's second language acquisition. In the field of syllabus design, negotiated (process) syllabuses proved to be applicable with young learners, and the outcome of the experiments has been measurably positive in many fields (Kelemen & Radnai, 1993; Radnai, 1994).

As to the pedagogical implications, Radnai (1996) states that an early start in foreign language learning is feasible and effective given the necessary conditions. The task and importance of further research in this field is to look into the possibilities of developing programmes which are applicable on a large scale, and produce standard, predictable results. In case of an early start, until reading and writing in the second language are introduced, the frequency of language sessions should be kept as high as possible, and their duration should be adjusted to the attention span and endurance of the learners. Reading and writing activities need more time, so their introduction demands new arrangements. Young learners need more help in analyzing and producing larger chunks of speech. Production tends to take place at a level (words and sentences) lower than reception. The implications for syllabus design are that more input on the text level is necessary, and that more attention needs to be paid to exercises and awareness-raising on the level of text and discourse. The earlier a second language is acquired, the more likely it becomes that another foreign language or more languages can be learned in the period of public education.

5.5   Proceedings in the workshops

During Workshop 4B, two groups covered the theme evaluation (Report on Workshop 4B, p. 56-67 and p. 68-77). After taking stock of the developments occurring within the timescale of Workshop 4A to 4B (see section 4) both groups started working on drawing up the practical principles governing evaluation and assessment at school level. The practical principles governing assessment, as stated by one group, can be described under the following headings.

Goal-related
Evaluation and assessment should be designed so as to provide information to various appropriate groups on the extent to which these goals are being achieved.

Integration in the processes of teaching and learning
Assessment should regularly and systematically be integrated into the processes of learning and teaching. That is, it should reflect the kinds of activity that regularly occur in class and with which pupils are familiar. It should have a strong diagnostic function

that will provide useful information to teachers and learners in enabling them to take stock of where they are and if necessary to adapt their particular strategies.

Readiness

Assessment should take place at times when pupils are ready to be assessed. There is for example little point in assessing children in domains that have not formed part of their curriculum to that point or that have been introduced but are still at a very initial and premature stage of development. Even when a domain has been in development for a lengthy period, it is likely that within classes there will be considerable variation in the extent to which particular pupils are ready at a given time. In consequence, assessment tasks may have to be spread over a period of time, to take account of the different rates and rhythms of learning within the class, rather than always be administered to all pupils at the one fixed time.

Record of progress

Assessment at primary school should consist of observing, analysing, describing and reporting on the progress of learners in the development of their proficiency in the foreign language and possibility of other constructs such as their attitude, their awareness of language and of culture and their personal development.

Positive account

Normally, assessment should be recorded positively, i.e. it should provide an account of what pupils have shown themselves able to do (rather than represent an inventory of failure). Information should be provided on: 1) the kinds of task that pupils are able to accomplish, 2) the modes of communication that they are able to adopt in doing so (listening, speaking, reading, writing, non-verbal), 3) the specific functions, notions, vocabulary and grammar activated (or mastered) in performing these tasks, 4) the conditions of achievement (eg context identical to / similar to / different from the original learning context; the extent to which support is provided by the teacher or others before and/or during the task), 5) the level of language at which they perform (taking account of factors such as range, fluency, accuracy, appropriateness, command of discourse, communication strategies).

A provisional framework for progression

Classroom teachers should possess a framework of descriptions of what pupils can do (or not do) at different stages in their foreign language development. This framework will necessarily incorporate a set of assumptions concerning progression in the foreign language. Without such assumptions, teachers will not be in a position to diagnose difficulties or to understand whether or not pupils are making progress. To some extent, the framework will consist of mental schemata that the teacher has internalized and can operate in everyday interactions with pupils, in order to make sense of the language and other performance of pupils; and to some extent it may consist of checklists that the teacher has compiled (possibly with the collaboration of national, regional or local groups) that enable pupil performance on particular sorts of task to be charted. It should be emphasized that this framework of assumptions concerning progression will always be provisional and subject to modification.

Explicit criteria, adapted to particular tasks

The above framework of descriptions, whether deriving from mental schemata or task-related checklists, should include explicit criteria for pupil performance, eg fluency, appropriateness range, accuracy. Normally, these criteria should be adapted to the particular tasks that pupils are attempting. For example, the criteria for participating in a 3-person conversation will be different from the criteria for telling a short story and different again from the criteria for understanding the teacher when she/he is talking in the foreign language.

Transparency of communication with other bodies

It will be important to be able to communicate information on pupils' progress appropriately to groups such as parents, other primary school staff, staff at secondary level, national and regional officials, politicians, teacher trainers, researchers and of course pupils themselves. These descriptions of pupil performance should be transparent enough for both specialists and non-specialists to understand and accept them as worthwhile. Of particular importance will be the communication of information to staff in secondary schools, providing them with a basis on which to help pupils develop further rather than make a fresh start. One single framework of descriptions for all of the above groups is unlikely to suffice. It is more likely that the descriptions will require to be adapted to suit the needs of each particular group.

Furthermore one workgroup produced the broad outlines of an illustrative framework for the evaluation of foreign language programs. The framework provides an indication of three important types of factor to be taken into account: input factors, process factors and outcome factors. The framework is illustrative only, in that for each set one would have to add many additional examples before a comprehensive list was established.

Diagram 1. An illustrative framework for programme evaluation foreign languages in primary schools

INPUTS →→→→→   PROCESS →→→→→→→→→   OUTCOMES
- Intended
- Unintended

Learners   **Learning**   **Learning Outcomes**
- Aptitude   - Learning strategies   - Proficiency
- Attitude   - Communication strategies   - Attitudes
- Ability   - Self-concept
- Personality   - Cultural awareness
                                                      - Language awareness
                                                      - General cognitive development

Teachers   **Teaching**   **Teacher Outcomes**
- Primary   - Degree of focus   - Degree of job
- Secondary   - Adaptability   satisfaction
                      - Choice of activities   - New insights & approaches
- Native Speaker   - Differentiation   approaches
- Non-Native Speaker   - Support for learners   - New contacts
                      - Commitment, patience,
- Trained for foreign   enthusiasm
    language teaching
- Level of proficiency

Resources   **Teacher Support**
- Equipment & materials   - Further training to meet new needs
- Number of teachers   - Support from senior management
- Rooms

School factors   **School Outcomes**
- State /Independent   - Curriculum change
- Socio-economic background   - Parental satisfaction
- Size of school/class   - Relations with secondaries
- Location (city, town, village)   - Links with schools abroad
- Ethos of school

Programme type   **Societal Outcomes**
- Foreign language as subject   - Number of foreign
- Embedding   language speakers
- Immersion   - Links with foreign
- Awareness   communities

Time for foreign language
- Duration & Intensity

Input factors at the start of the programme describe what the situation is like, eg. a school's socio-economic status. Process factors represent what occurs as the program is implemented. Clearly, teachers will be integral to many different sorts of process; pupils too, but also senior staff in schools and others including parents. Process factors can be particularly difficult to identify and understand, since many of the most important processes occurring in classrooms (ie. those happening inside people's heads) are not directly observable. Outcome factors represent the different constructs one may wish to bear in mind in order to make a judgement as to the program outcome. Outcome factors are for example learning results, in terms of pupils' command of the language or their attitudes. But one may also think of outcomes in relation to teachers, schools and society.

A cursory glance at the framework makes two things clear: 1) different combinations of input and process factors may lead to very different sorts of outcomes, and 2) the relationships between these input, process and outcome factors are highly complex and difficult to understand.

5.6   Specific needs for evaluation and assessment

In most European countries FLE is still in a 'pilot phase' (Edelenbos & Koster, 1994). Within a few years FLE will go into a new phase that probably can be typified as the 'consolidation phase'. This statement is made from the perspective that FLE, without reasonable doubt, will become a well established part of the primary curriculum. However, the 'consolidation phase' has several inherent threats. At this stage an abundance of positive energy is being put into innovating and stimulating developments to make FLE work. As soon as FLE has been more or less accepted and integrated in the primary curriculum those energetic drives will diminish and gradually a state of equilibrium will be reached. During this consolidation phase questions with regard to the outcomes for pupils, schools and society will be raised. FLE will not be excluded from this drive for accountability because a) FLE takes up precious teaching and learning time, b) results, in terms of overt assessable learning results for future life, are still hard to grasp (compare with mathematics) and c) the problem of continuity into secondary education is not yet solved in an adequate way.

So, there are specific needs for evaluation and assessment during this consolidation phase. A very broad range of topics for evaluation could be identified. In the light of the above mentioned problems during the perceived consolidation phase two essential themes for evaluation and assessment deserve further consideration.

i)   Effective foreign language teaching

There is much pressure on the primary school curriculum, and teaching-time can only be spent once. One only has to look at the increasing impact of computers in daily life and the necessity for pupils to operate them, to understand that in the near future teaching-time will become even more scarce. For subjects such as mathematics the

73

search for crucial variables in effective teaching has been going on for years. The implications of determining effective foreign language teaching for policy-making, curriculum development and teacher education are evident. A convincing, overall, research-based model of 'effective foreign-language teaching' that incorporates essential characteristics such as 'time for learning' and 'time on task' (Carroll, 1989) still has to find its place in research publications on foreign-language learning, though there have been many studies on particular aspects. To existing models for effective teaching (Creemers, 1994) should be added characteristics that are specific to modern foreign or second languages, because such models do not reach the heart of foreign-language teaching: the learning process. The strategies, techniques and mental operations that take place in the learning process influence the opportunities to learn and in the end effect the learner's competence and proficiency in the foreign language. However, characteristics at several levels are identified by Edelenbos & Johnstone (1996, p. 74 ff) that could be incorporated in future models for effective foreign language teaching.

At *the school level* the following characteristics might be of influence: Appropriate, shared ethos and values among staff, parents and pupils, good communications among staff, strong policy for liaison between primary & secondary, setting of high expectations and standards, capability for self-evaluation, sufficient time and opportunity made available for learning and using the foreign language by teachers and pupils.

At *the curriculum level* the following characteristics might be of importance: syllabus that takes account of national, local and individual needs, learning a foreign language not only as subject but also used as means of learning other subject-matter, materials and approaches that provide advance organisers, appropriate grouping, differentiation, corrective instruction, feedback, evaluation.

Teacher characteristics that might be of influence are: creation of relaxed, enjoyable and work-oriented atmosphere in which the foreign language is consistently used, engaging pupils in dialogue so as to help them develop appropriate learner strategies in keeping with their age and stage of development, and purposes in learning, making clear what pupils are to do, helping them with their work, maximising their time-on-task.

At *the pupil level* one may identify: aptitude for foreign language learning, general cognitive ability, level of first language literacy, level of meta-linguistic awareness, positive attitudes and motivation for foreign language learning and use and awareness of appropriate strategies for foreign language learning. Characteristics of learner support out of school are parents and others who support the school's values, facilities and encouragement at home for study and socio-economic background of the family.

The impact of these characteristics on each other will work out in different ways in different countries. In some countries, for example, societal attitudes to the learning of a particular foreign language will be so strong and positive that pupils will learn the language (to some extent at least) whether or not the schools or the teaching are particularly effective. In other countries on the other hand, where societal attitudes are less strong and where there is considerably less exposure to and use of the foreign language, the role of effective schools and teaching will be crucial in helping to create appropriate levels of attitude and motivation that might otherwise not be there.

ii) The continuity into secondary education

As stated in section 5.4 the continuity problem will present itself in different shapes throughout Europe, but five elements can be identified: an information/communication gap, lack of fine-tuning in aims and goals (at several intermediate stages), differences in didactical approaches and subject matter, reluctancy at the secondary level to acknowledge the learning results at the primary level and shortcomings in initial and in-service training to address the above-mentioned problems. At national levels and a supra national level, studies into the continuity into secondary education are needed. On the one hand, evaluations could be conducted to establish the causes of the problem and the strength of the problem, and on the other hand small scale studies could be set up to investigate the effects of possible solutions i.e. establishing functional communication patterns between the primary and secondary sectors, clarifying and fine tuning of goals, fine tuning of approaches to foreign language teaching and learning in both types of schools and mutual in-service training of teachers in primary and secondary education.

5.7 Instruction and learning processess

The complexity of the contexts that have to be taken into account means that much of the future evaluations and assessments should be undertaken by trained, expert researchers, but they will have to abandon the role of distant observers in favour of that of skilful gatherers of information, dealing with complex and changing educational systems. There could be a role for action-research based on collaborative groups that include classroom practitioners who have an interest in innovating aspects of their own practice. The place, functions and goals of evaluations and assessments with a strong empirical background, however, differs from unstructured and uncontrolled work within collaborative groups.

Evaluations and assessments related to the work that has been done in international workshops organized by the Council of Europe and related research and development programs, have not uncovered the success of innovating approaches to teaching and learning foreign languages in primary schools. This is not due to the work done. In the last decade very few studies have been carried out into this very complex area, because funding for essential fundamental research into innovating approaches to teaching and learning foreign languages has been rather meager.

The outcomes of the Educational Research Workshop on the effectiveness of foreign language learning and teaching organized by the Council of Europe in Graz (Austria), underline the need for research into this field. During this workshop, three essential areas were identified in which extensive educational research into foreign language learning and teaching is needed. In the first place, research is absolutely necessary into the way languages are learnt by pupils in schools. In the second place, research has to identify the factors that influence language learners and their learning, such as

75

psychological factors, the difficulty of tasks, the arrangements in the learning environment and active engagement in learning tasks. In the third place, research is needed into the relationship between teaching and learning. What should be uncovered is what is going on in the classroom and how instruction and classroom interaction influences learning processess and individual differences in learning a foreign language. Research into effective foreign language teaching in primary schools as described in section 5 could give an extra dimension to these three areas of vital importance.

6. TEACHER EDUCATION
Maria FELBERBAUER - Austria

6.1 Background

"In view of the necessity of introducing foreign language education into the
primary schools of all European countries, we believe that one of the conditions
to be fulfilled is the supply of suitably qualified teachers"
(Report on Workshop 8B, 134).

Quite obviously, the success or failure of all programmes for learning foreign languages
at primary level depends on the quality of the teachers. At present teachers come from
within the primary or the secondary sector. This effects the weightings of their linguistic
or pedagogical training.

Secondary school teachers are usually experts in foreign language teaching. Their
training must concentrate on how to combine foreign language teaching with primary
methodology. Priorities and accepted practices must be reviewed and additional
competence in certain areas has to be acquired. Secondary school language teachers
must learn to approach the language in a more natural and spontaneous way, to rely on
the skills of listening and speaking, and to use fun activities preferred by very young
learners, such as children's rhymes, songs, language games, chants and stories.

Primary school teachers, who are experts in primary school methodology, may lack
linguistic competence. If they belong to the group of "ab initio" language learners
training them will be possible only at great expense. If they have limited, average or
advanced linguistic skills they need training programmes which are geared to their
individual requirements.

Lately, international organisations have recommended a greater diversification of
languages at all levels. Therefore educational authorities will try to offer more than one
foreign language at primary schools so the development of effective training
programmes becomes even more important.

6.2 Developing the concept

In order to develop a general concept for training teachers, the *Modern Languages
Section of the Council of Europe* initiated the international workshops mentioned in the
introduction. Discussions among the participants pointed out that national contexts differ
widely with regard to the language competence, methodological background, cultural
awareness and attitudinal disposition of the prospective teachers. Therefore workshop

participants decided that internationally applicable concepts should be as comprehensible as possible and, at the same time, guarantee flexibility and adaptability.

The first idea was to develop a modular training programme. Its advantages are quite obvious: Whenever national authorities decide to include a foreign language in the primary curriculum, they study the programme, determine the range of competences the teachers already have, select certain modules, ignore others and put together their own individual training courses.

However, after studying the results of the work of several workshops, it becomes obvious that this initial idea was never fully realised. Experts seem to have learnt that qualifying as a foreign language teacher for primary school requires more than achieving a certain level of linguistic and methodological competence. Languages cannot not be separated from their cultural background. It is therefore necessary to combine linguistic skills with intercultural knowledge. This process may trigger a reconsideration of one's own attitudes towards a multicultural society, it may mean abandoning prejudices, avoiding stereotypes and accepting cultural differences. Becoming a teacher of foreign languages is a process which requires professional **and** personal involvement. It may change one's personal outlook and add a multi-cultural perspective to a teacher's professional qualifications. Concepts that were developed by the participants of workshops or by experts in Research and Development Networks between two "New Style" Workshops, reflect this idea. There are also other areas of general consent.

Experts agree that teacher education in modern languages can be started at pre- or in-service level. At present, the need for qualified teachers in many countries can only be met by in-service training institutions. In the long run, universities and colleges must offer initial training programmes for all prospective primary school teachers. These pre-service courses should be supplemented throughout the teacher's professional career by in-service training programmes. It is advisable to spend a period of time in the target language country.

Successful foreign language teaching at primary level depends on the ability of the teachers to link it with the primary curriculum. They must observe the general criteria for good primary education. Foreign language teaching at primary level has to be child- and needs-oriented, holistic and communicative, experiential, playful, intercultural, authentic and autonomous. Only if teacher education succeeds in making these goals transparent, will teachers become "specialists both in primary education and foreign language pedagogy" (Report on Workshop 8B, 134).

More specifically, teachers must learn to use the classroom situation for language learning purposes. Primary school children are not as target oriented as older pupils. They react spontaneously and sometimes want to change quickly from one activity to the next, but are willing to remain for any length of time at a task which most adults would consider boring. They have a great natural curiosity, can be very talkative, are willing to accept another identity and act out little scenes. Their receptive skills can be trained by using the foreign language for classroom management and organisation.

Materials and resources used in general teaching can be adapted for foreign language learning purposes and help to integrate the new subject into everyday classroom work. Language learning processes tend to stretch over long periods, sometimes over a lifetime of learning. Such dimensions are incomprehensible and frightening for young children and may lead to discouragement. The language teacher at the primary level must therefore try to convey the impression that each step in the language learning process, no matter how small, is a real achievement.

Generally it is suggested that teacher education be "a combination of theory, awareness-raising activities, experiential activities, demonstration activities, personal study and research and, if possible, provision of feed-back about the performance in class" (Report on Workshop 4B, 82).

6.3 Defining the principles

"Teacher Education is a permanent process of professional learning geared to the needs both of the individual and the educational system and school" (Report on Workshop 8B, 135).

No matter which institution is responsible for it, training should take into account "the different previous learning experiences" (Report on Workshop 4B, 81) of the trainees. Most teacher students and school teachers will have no former experience of learning a foreign language at primary level. Some of them may have had an unsuccessful and unenjoyable foreign language learning experience in the past. It may not be easy to realise that language learning can be a pleasant and rewarding experience. For in-service teachers, in particular, it may be difficult to develop self confidence in a field where they feel out of their depth. This calls for great sensitivity on the part of the trainer.

Obviously "the different preferred learning styles of the teachers and their varied and various expectations of approaches and content of the training programme" (Report on Workshop 4B, 81) will have to be taken into account. If the training programme does not meet expectations, a teacher's motivation to learn new techniques will be minimal. Later on such a teacher may not feel inclined to motivate his young learners.

It is very important that participants be encouraged to exploit their expertise in primary methodology and/or language competence. Such insights should be shared mutually with the other members of the training programme. This procedure helps to raise the level of confidence trainees may have with regard to improving their knowledge of a foreign language and culture.

6.4 Determining the aims

If we approach the question of aims in a pragmatic, "language-based" way, we will agree with Alison Hurrell, who claimed that training should include:

- language learning aims
- methodological aims
- attitudinal aims (Workshop 17 - Texts of the Animators).

Obviously these categories are applicable for an in-service rather than a pre-service training situation. General aims in the fields of psychology, education or primary school pedagogy are not included, because they are not part of in-service training.

The participants of Workshop 8B, who developed a model for pre-service training, took a more comprehensive outlook and grouped the aims as follows:

- knowledge
- attitudes
- competences (Report on Workshop 8B, 135).

The following summary is an attempt to draw the the two positions together. For the sake of clarity and applicability the "language-based" approach was given preference to serve as a general framework.

Language learning aims include knowledge in general linguistics, socio- and psycho-linguistics, in the development of language(s), language learner strategies and learning styles.

Primary school language teachers must aim at an excellent standard of articulation and be especially competent in the skills of listening and speaking.

In addition they must be competent in specific language areas for primary schools:

- the language for classroom interaction and management,
- the language for communicative purposes,
- the language of games, songs, rhymes and story telling,
- the language for the delivery of cross curricular activities,
- the language for the personal linguistic resource of the teacher.

Methodological aims range from the development of professional skills and attitudes to creating appropriate language learning situations in the primary classroom. Essential teaching strategies like asking real questions, adapting the language level to the needs of the learners, explaining new words and phrases verbally and nonverbally, encouraging the pupils by means of positive feedback, organising activity based language teaching, applying a multi-sensory approach, developing strategies for embedding the foreign language in the primary curriculum, etc. will be required.

Teachers must learn to adapt resources and materials, use media and handle texts that are suitable for the age group.

Attitudinal aims concern the teacher's personal attitudes towards his own and towards the foreign culture. The teacher should learn to respect and tolerate cultural diversity, avoid stereotypes and practice empathy.

6.5   Finding the methods

"The methods of initial teacher education and in-service teacher education have a common basis. They must be self-directed, theory-led, practice rooted."
(Report on Workshop 8B, 146).

There is common agreement that in successful teacher training, theory and practice play equally important parts. There are certain differences in intensity and distribution. In pre-service training, foreign language education will be one of the areas among many others, where student teachers can develop individual teaching styles. The language part of the lessons will serve as a basis for trying out teaching techniques. In an in-service situation the trainee knows the methods and has the opportunity to concentrate on the language part of the lesson. The following graphs illustrate the importance of the interrelationship between theory and practice. The first model was developed at Workshop 8B for pre-service training. The second model was devised at Workshop 8A for in-service purposes.

The reflective model for initial teacher training (Report on Workshop 8B, 146)
The students' practical classroom work is theory based, and this theoretical knowledge is modified by their classroom experience (——————>). In their school practicum they receive stimuli for their theoretical work, which in due course have an effect on their classroom performance (--------------->).

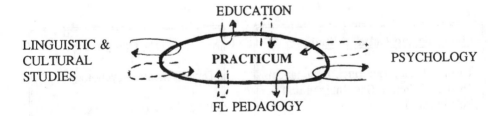

The in-service training model (Report on Workshop 8A, 87)

course 1 ⇒ practice
          (feedback) ⇒ course 2 ⇒ practice
                     (feedback) ⇒ course 3 ⇒ ⇒ ⇒

The model was considered applicable for for two groups of teachers:

- those with some training in a foreign language and/or language competence
- those trained in a foreign language, but with no working experience in primary school   (e.g. only experience in secondary school).

6.6 Describing the contents

After Workshop 8A, a group of teachers and teacher trainers from nine European countries began to work on an optimal model for teacher education. The work was finalised during an interim meeting between Workshop 8A and 8B in Prague. The model is therefore called the *Prague Model*. On account of its structure it is applicable in many contexts and contains a detailed description of all the elements that can be included in a training programme.

The Prague Model

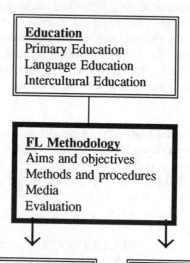

Education
Primary Education
Language Education
Intercultural Education

FL Methodology
Aims and objectives
Methods and procedures
Media
Evaluation

Linguistic and Cultural Studies

Theory of Language (incl. Pragmatics)
Theory of Culture (inc. Intercultural
Relationship)

L2 :   Grammar
Lexicology
Phonology

Psychology

Developmental Psychology

Psychology of Learning

Social Psychology

Psycholinguistics

In the following list of items the boxes of the Prague Model are specified in detail.

```
┌──────────────────────────────┐
│  Education                   │
│                              │
│  Primary Education           │
│  Language Education          │
│  Intercultural Education     │
│                              │
└──────────────────────────────┘
```

- The role of primary education within the education system as a whole
- Purposes of primary education
- Primary school methods
- L1 and L2 education in the primary school - mutual support and co-operation
- The necessity of foreign language education at the primary level
- The aims and methods of intercultural education
- The integration of FL education into the primary school curriculum
- Classroom management
- Classroom research - strategies and methods

```
┌──────────────────────────────────┐
│  Foreign Language Methodology    │
│  Aims and objectives             │
│  Methods and procedures          │
│  Media                           │
│  Evaluation                      │
│                                  │
└──────────────────────────────────┘
```

- Communicative competence as the overall aim
- Awareness of one's first language and of the possibility to communicate by other means
- The four communicative skills and their interrelationship
- The linguistic and cultural contents of foreign language education
- Content-based instruction
- The explanation of meaning
- The teaching of linguistic form(s): implicit grammar, pronunciation
- Holistic and multisensory approaches
- Specific procedures: fun activities, games, role plays, phantasy trips, imagination exercises, storytelling
- Overview of the media available and their usability in FL education
- Characteristics of the media and their suitability in the various educational contexts
- Evaluation - its forms and functions; its importance for the assessment of learning, irrespective of formal marking
- Cross-curricular teaching
- Interactive teaching / learning
- The planning of foreign language lessons

> **Linguistic and Cultural Studies**
>
> Theory of Language (incl. Pragmatics)
> Theory of Culture (inc. Intercultural
> Relationship)
>
> L2 : Grammar
>   Lexicology
>   Phonology

- Language as a system of signs
- The function of language
- Competence and performance, varieties, dialects, sociolects
- Culture „as a way of life"
- Linguistic knowledge and skills in the target language: pronunciation, lexis and syntax
- Intercultural awareness and respect for cultural diversity
- Knowledge of and insight into the culture of the country or countries where the target language is used as the mother tongue
- Difficulties in intercultural communication and the possible means of overcoming them
- Relationship between first language and second / foreign language

> **Psychology**
>
> Developmental Psychology
>
> Psychology of Learning
>
> Social Psychology
>
> Psycholinguistics

- Human development
- Development of L1 and L2
- Development of (inter)cultural awareness
- Conditions and ways of learning
- First and second / foreign language learning, the relationship between the two
- Positive and negative transfer
- Bilingualism
- Interlanguage
- Human behaviour in relationship to other persons, groups and society as a whole
- Stereotypes, prejudices and discrimination

6.7 Conclusion

Foreign language teaching is one of the main mediators for intercultural education, and for this reason the person teaching the foreign language should also be the class teacher, who should receive an adequate qualification in foreign language pedagogy. In due course, all prospective teachers should receive initial training in the field of foreign language education.

However, pre-service courses should be supplemented by in-service training in order to guarantee that teachers

- can work on their language competence,
- are informed about new methods in foreign language education,
- have the opportunity to exchange materials and develop new concepts,
- can participate in exchange programmes so that they can adapt their attitudes, knowledge and skills with respect to intercultural education ,
- share, explore and develop ideas on how to promote the principle of continuity in foreign language education together with secondary school teachers.

Changes in educational policies are never successful when attempted half-heartedly. Introducing a foreign language in primary schools without initiating an adequate programme of pre- and in-service teacher education would mean just that. The participants of Workshop 8B made this very clear when they accepted the following text as final resolution:

"An effective, integrated programme of initial and in-service teacher training is essential to the proper development of modern language teaching in primary schools. Specialised training in primary methodology should be combined with steps to ensure that teachers have the specialised language competence necessary to teach effectively using the foreign language according to the methods being used in these schools. Continuing staff development should also be provided including the promotion of teacher co-operation and networking across disciplinary and sector boundaries." (Report on Workshop 8B, 156).

CONCLUSIONS
Peter DOYÉ and Alison HURRELL

At Workshop 8A one of the seven working groups attempted a survey of approaches to foreign language education in primary schools. This group took up the seven basic questions with which all teachers, curriculum-planners and policy makers are faced today and formulated these in the form of seven dichotomies.

- Integration   vs   Separate Subject
- Language Learning   vs   Linguistic and Cultural Awareness
- Communicative Competence   vs   Sensitisation
- Systematic Course   vs   Occasional Teaching
- Form Teacher   vs   Subject Teacher
- Primary Education   vs   Pre-Secondary Education
- Part of the Core Curriculum   vs   Optional Activity

Manuel TOST PLANET has taken up six of these dichotomies in his fundamental chapter of this compendium and has demonstrated how useful they can be as guidelines for defining the objectives and content of teaching programmes for young learners of the foreign language.

Useful they are indeed, as they present in concise form a series of seven binary hypotheses for discussion. In our conclusions, on the basis of (a) the work done at, and between, the five Workshops and (b) the reflections of the contributors to this compendium, we aim to provide answers which are less tentative, though not prescriptive, and identify the controversies which still exist.

We will therefore use these dichotomies to draw the threads of each of the six chapters together, to highlight areas of consensus and, where they arise, areas of divergence of opinion, in order to provide answers to the questions raised within each of the dichotomies.

1. Integration *vs* Separate Subject

What is immediately striking about the six contributions is the degree of consensus about this and other matters pertaining to foreign languages in primary education. In Chapter 1, Manuel Tost Planet reminds us that primary education is, or should be, child-centred, in the sense that learning objectives and their translation into curricular areas should respond to the learning needs, the learning styles and the interests of the young child, and should take full cognisance of the intellectual, affective and social development of each child. In Chapter 4, Hanna KOMOROWSKA stresses the operational and motivational advantages of integrating the foreign language into the primary curriculum. *Inter alia* integration allows children to relate the foreign language to concepts about the world that they already possess or that they are actually learning at school. The foreign language can be coordinated with these existing concepts, thus promoting a holistic approach to learning. It helps children learn how to learn by supporting cognitive strategies. It enables the class teacher to help the children make connections between the language(s) they already possess and the foreign language they are learning. It encourages the view that the purpose of learning a foreign language is not just to learn the language but also to experience or learn something about life through the language.

In Chapter 2, Lisbeth YTREBERG outlines some of the potential disadvantages of integrating the foreign language into the primary curriculum, thereby identifying a potential area for future research and development. In essence, she states that almost by definition, the embedding model is linguistically diffuse. It does not teach a pre-defined body of language containing its own built-in progression of vocabulary, grammar and function, as the subject model does. There is a danger that this can lead to a rather fragmented approach, where the class teacher is making links between the foreign language and mathematics one week, between the foreign language and environmental studies the next. The obvious problems remain - how the class teacher keeps track of the various new language items, how he/she ensures recycling, consolidation, progression and continuity, and how the language system is internalised by the children in a coherent and cohesive way. Another concern must be the built-in discontinuity of approach between the primary and the secondary sector, where in many countries the model of foreign language provision at secondary level remains one of discrete subject teaching. This can pose particular problems for language teachers at secondary schools and indeed for the pupils as they move into the secondary sector with a considerable body of foreign language at their disposal. Unless the secondary teacher can tap this reservoir of foreign language competence and build on positive attitudes to the acquisition of the foreign language, the pupils become frustrated, demotivated and disaffected.

Is there a sustainable argument for teaching a foreign language as a separate subject? Many have argued for a return to the traditional notion of the subject-model with a clearly pre-defined linear teaching programme, with its own body of knowledge, its own distinctive aims and its own teaching and learning processes that differentiate it from other subjects. This, they argue, can be delivered in ways which are nonetheless consonant with the ways in which children learn in other areas of the primary curriculum. However, the curriculum in most European primary schools is organised holistically on the basis of broad areas of study and an introduction of the subject model would be in opposition to this holistic organisation.

2. Language learning *vs* Linguistic and Cultural Awaress

The second dichotomy represents indeed one of the basic questions of FLE in the primary school, maybe the basic question, and the experts assembled at the 5 Council of Europe workshops have given a clear answer to it: FLE has to be both - language learning and the acquisition of linguistic and cultural awareness.

On the one hand, FLE can no longer be restricted to language learning proper, and its purpose cannot be the acquisition of linguistic competence (in the narrow sense) alone. It must try to contribute to the wider task of developing an intercultural communicative competence and has therefore to include linguistic and cultural awareness. On the other hand, such an awareness would be useless without the learning of other languages.

On the basis of van Ek's analyses (van Ek, 1986), Byram and Zarate have presented a very lucid description of intercultural communicative competence and have shown that it has at least three dimensions, a pragmatic, a cognitive and an attitudinal dimension.

They speak of

- savoir-faire   (skills)
- savoir   (knowledge) and
- savoir-être   (attitudes);

and they have suggested that any foreign langugage teaching today should comprise these three dimensions.

The European experts on primary foreign language education seem to agree that what is true of FLE in general can, with justification, also be said of FLE at the primary in particular. In the early projects, primary school teachers concentrated on enabling their children to gain linguistic competence. They aimed at a certain level of achievement in the basic skills such as listening comprehension and speaking and at a later stage, reading comprehension and writing; and if the children were able to produce well-formed utterances in the foreign language and to understand such utterances, this was regarded as satisfactory. Little or no attention was paid to the cognitive and attitudinal dimension. But a better understanding of communicative competence and the changes in the political reality of our modern world have led to a different concept of the purpose of primary FLE.

For many young children, contact with members of other cultures is no longer an event that might occur in the distant future, but an immediate possibility in their present-day lives. They actually meet people of a foreign culture and therefore with a foreign language and consequently have to learn to cope with the situations arising out of such encounters. It is the duty of the school and of FLE in particular to help them in their learning, i.e. in the acquisition of the required skills, knowledge and attitudes.

3. Communicative Competence *vs* Sensitisation

In Chapter 1, Manuel Tost Planet provides us with a working definition of sensitisation, highlighting the general nature of the aims and objectives of this approach: to sensitize children more generally to the nature, purposes and structure of language (language awareness) or to aspects of the cultures in which particular languages are spoken (cultural awareness). It does not aim primarily to develop communicative competence in an additional language. In his book *Awareness of Language: an introduction* (1984) Eric Hawkins stresses the importance of the child's own culture and first language as the basis for comparison with those elsewhere. An assumption underlying this approach is that children's understanding of the concept of 'language' will be strengthened if the concept is approached through a number of languages rather than one language alone. Sensitisation can be regarded as educationally desirable in itself or indeed can go hand-in-hand with foreign language learning.

In Chapter 2, Lisbeth Ytreberg gives us examples of methodological features which appear as part and parcel of a communicative approach to the teaching and learning of a foreign language. Since the late 1970s it is safe to say that communicative competence has generally been acknowledged as the aim of foreign language teaching programmes in both sectors. That is, the capacity to adapt to the contextual demands of a situation and to use a stock of language to receive and send appropriate messages. In other words, people will want to communicate when they have a purpose in so doing or when they perceive the need to do so. Communication implies a genuine exchange of information, language learning 'for real' not merely 'for practice'. It also implies that a resource of language has to be amassed, from which the children can select appropriately to express their needs, wishes and desires. It implies moreover that they can cope with the unpredictable; firstly in understanding what has been said or written and secondly in selecting something appropriate to say in response. The term 'communicative competence' describes the system of rules and strategies that learners must be able to exploit if they are to use a language for real communication. Van Ek (1986) has identified six components of communicative competence:

- linguistic competence
- sociolinguistic competence
- discourse competence
- strategic competence
- sociocultural competence and
- social competence

Although busy classrooms are not the best contexts for a full realisation of these components, primary school teachers are at least in a favourable position to lay the foundations for children's competence in all these areas. How the six components can be integrated into an overall communicative competence is a question of method, and Lisbeth Ytreberg has summarised the respective proposals of European experts in Chapter 2. But it is definitely <u>competence</u> which teachers have to aim at. There seems to be general agreement that <u>sensitisation</u> is not enough.

90

To make children aware of the nature of language, of its structure and its functions in the life of human beings, can be a valuable first step in language acquisition and is therefore desirable also in primary foreign language education. But this first step is not sufficient in itself. The dispositions and motivations of primary school children and the present socio-political situation in Europe require more: the laying of a solid foundation of communicative competence in a foreign language. This foundation (for restrictive curricular reasons) will have to be limited in many primary school contexts, but it must certainly go beyond mere sensitisation.

4. Systematic Course *vs* Occasional Teaching

Amongst the variables quoted by Peter EDELENBOS in his diagram on page 72 two are of particular importance here: **programme type** and **time for foreign language.** By systematic course is meant a teaching and learning programme in which the following have been defined, articulated and elaborated in order to create a **cohesive, coherent** and **progressive** whole:

- objectives and content
- methods
- resources
- evaluation and assessment

B.P.M. Creemers (1994) stated that, "Time for learning is the key factor for educational effectiveness. Quality of instruction also contributes to the effectiveness of education". (*'The Effective Classroom'* as quoted in *"Researching Languages at Primary School - Some European Perspectives"* edited by Peter Edelenbos and Richard Johnstone). He identified the following *inter alia* as characteristics of effective teaching:

1. The quality of instruction in the curriculum, which included the explicitness and ordering of goals and content, the structure and clarity of content, and frequent use of evaluation techniques.

2. Time for learning which seems to be the most reliable predictive classroom-related factor for explaining differences in pupils' performance in foreign language learning

3. Grouping procedures, which stress cooperative learning dependent on differentiated material

4. Teacher behaviour

5. Time on task

If we consider these five characteristics in the broader context of effective foreign language learning, recent research, the 5 Council of Europe workshops dedicated to foreign language learning in primary education, and, indeed, classroom-based development in a variety of local and national contexts, have much to tell us. Chapter 1 deals extensively with aims and content and Chapters 4 and 5 stress the need for regular and systematic assessment as an integral part of the teaching and learning process, reflecting the kinds of activity that regularly occur in class and with which the children are familiar. The diagnostic importance of evaluation and assessment is also stressed, a diagnosis which will provide timely and effective feedback to pupils and teachers, and information on the children's progress to teachers in both sectors, to parents and other interested parties. A systematic course will ensure this characteristic of effective teaching and learning.

In her chapter on Methods, Lisbeth Ytreberg states that there is no place for the explicit teaching of grammar in primary foreign language teaching programmes. The teacher's main concern will be to identify a range of language which contains simplified syntax and a vocabulary which is accessible without being unnatural. However, recent research in Hungary, quoted in Chapter 5, would indicate that young learners of a foreign language (with existing competence in their first language) are capable of analysis and synthesis and that long-term developmental strategies can be planned by the class teacher, where the children have the opportunity to reflect on their knowledge of the language. Without a systematic and structured introduction to the various components of communicative competence outlined by van Ek, we may run the risk of never exploiting the children's knowledge of their first language and never developing their ability to internalise the system of rules and strategies which govern communicative competence. We may wish to consider a role for explicit knowledge about language, including grammar, to promote accuracy in addition to fluency and here we consider the role of knowledge about language to promote more accurate comprehension. The foreign language is acquired through a **gradual developmental process** that focuses both on **meaningful communicative activities** combined with **awareness-raising** and a **focus on the language system itself,** enabling the children to refine their understanding of the rules of the language. The length of time devoted to the teaching and learning of the foreign language is of course crucial here to our understanding of the issues surrounding the 'formal' teaching of knowledge about language. However, this is not to deny the importance of the natural approach on which most foreign language teaching programmes in primary education are predicated Whatever conclusions are reached at local and national levels about the introduction (or not) of formal learning, they will be based on evidence from research and the growing body of information we have about the ways in which young children acquire a foreign language.

The characteristic feature of time for learning can be looked at from two perspectives - that of when to start teaching a foreign language, and the frequency of the children's exposure to the foreign language. There is considerable consensus now about the desirability of an early start (5/6 - 10/11) based on the seemingly intrinsic capacity of the young learner to acquire the sound system of the language, their low 'affective filter', their enthusiasm and capacity for enjoyment, and their willingness to take risks and make errors work for them. In Chapter 5, Peter Edelenbos quotes recent research in Hungary where the highest correlation between pupil performance and time factors was to be found in the actual number of classroom hours spent learning the language. The frequency of the lessons also played an important role, certainly before reading and writing were introduced. These findings again were based on systematic teaching programmes and not on occasional teaching.

Grouping procedures are equally dealt with in Chapter 4 where Hanna Komorowska draws our attention to the increasing need at primary and at secondary level for pair work and team work to take account of the differentiated needs of the pupils as they develop their foreign language competence, to respond to remediation and extension needs of pupils. This may well take the form of differentiated materials and in Chapter 3, Rita BALBI highlights the usefulness of supplementary materials for the busy classroom teacher intent on providing differentiated support to his/her pupils. Recent research in Scotland (*"What's the Difference? A Study of Differentiation in Scottish Secondary Schools"* M. Simpson and J. Ure 1993) has indicated that one of the most effective means of differentiation is through dialogue with the pupils themselves. The key to effective differentiation was found to be the quality of interaction among participants, rather than to recourse to varying materials. This would seem to imply that teacher intervention makes a difference, perhaps occasionally extracting a small group with which to work more extensively. When the pupils' perspective about effective teaching was canvassed, the resounding conclusion was that the most important mediator of the children's success was the teacher: the teacher who acknowledged and signalled success and areas of weakness, who responded rapidly to the children's requests for assistance and who provided regular and effective feedback, mapping out 'next steps', sharing strategies for effective learning, maintaining high expectations of each pupil, setting clear goals and sharing the criteria for successful mastery of the learning outcomes. And all of this within the framework of a systematic teaching programme.

Throughout the deliberations of the 5 workshops and the research and development work undertaken in the interim, there would seem to be an almost universal consensus that children should acquire communicative competence through a structured, systematic approach to their learning, in terms of aims and content, appropriate methodologies, evaluation and assessment.

5. Form Teacher *vs* Subject Teacher

If it is generally accepted that integrating the foreign language into aspects of the primary curriculum is a *desideratum*, it then follows that the person best placed to do this is the class teacher. Primary education is child-centred education in the sense that pedagogical aims and teaching content are constructed around the interests and needs of the child and take into account his/her intellectual, emotional and social development. The primary school teacher, and more specifically, the class teacher, is one of the key figures in the learner's developmental process. As Franz Schimek said at Workshop 8A the class teacher is, "the one who truly has this unique opportunity to initiate that important first contact between the pupils and the foreign language". However, as Hanna Komorowska points out in Chapter 4, if a class teacher is implementing the idea of integration and embedding, then it presupposes a competent speaker of the foreign language with knowledge and understanding of appropriate methodologies. Moreover, such approaches will only be possible where there is an adequate supply of appropriately trained and qualified teachers. In Chapter 6 of this compendium (Teacher Education) Maria FELBERBAUER prefaces her definition of working principles and practices by highlighting, not only the level of linguistic and methodological competence required by the primary class teacher, but also the degree of intercultural knowledge required. This 'knowledge' subsumes an intercultural disposition, a willingness and capacity on the part of the teacher to respect and tolerate cultural diversity, to avoid stereotypes and to practise empathy.

The crux of the matter seems to lie in the statement 'an adequate supply of appropriately trained class teachers'. In the short-term, where there is not an adequate supply, it may simply not be possible for the teaching programmes to be delivered by the class teacher. In these instances a trained colleague may have to intervene on a drop-in basis, collaborating wherever possible with the class teacher to ensure that links are made with the rest of the primary curriculum an the ongoing work of the children. In-service training, focussing on foreign language skills and methodological skills, is seen as a pragmatic solution to an issue which continues to tax the minds and budgets of decision-makers in member countries. However, in-service training cannot be the definitive solution to the problem. As Maria Felberbauer states, "In due course all prospective teachers should receive initial training in the field of foreign language education."

6. Primary Education *vs* Pre-Secondary Education

With respect to this dichotomy, the participants of the five European workshops have reached considerable agreement. The consensus can be described as follows:

The primary school is an institution in its own right. It represents a first phase of schooling and a very important one. In primary education the foundations are laid for a great many fields of learning and for basic skills and strategies. That they are basic and that their promotion has to be continued at the secondary level of schooling is obvious; but they have a value in themselves. They have to be oriented to the child's needs and must be useful and meaningful.

This fundamental principle also applies to FLE, if it is introduced into the primary school. The learning of the foreign language will have to be basic, but not just preparatory for something that comes later. Ana Vivet has paid special attention to this aspect and reminded us of the necessity of remaining aware of the relevance of FLE to the young children themselves :

"What does it mean to children of 7 or 10 years of age to discover another language? What do children feel when they discover not only another way of speaking and communicating but also another culture with other values and symbols? Can we say that the learning of languages is positive for their development?" (Vivet 1995).

These are highly relevant questions and should always be considered in the planning of FLE. To conclude, one particular warning might not be amiss. However strong a position the protagonists of FLE at the primay level might wish to give it, this position will always be less strong than that of FLE at the secondary level - for obvious curricular reasons. In other words: The main part of FLE will always take place in the secondary school. But this must not lead to the fallacious conclusion that the primary stage is of minor importance and only a preparation for the "real" thing that comes later.

The statement of the continuity group at Workshop 4B is justified, "Teaching a foreign language in primary schools is not an end in itself. It must enable the child to benefit from the teaching at secondary level and ensure that this teaching has a greater impact and is more effective." (1993, p. 98). However this does not mean that primary FLE has to derive its justification from the desirability of improving secondary FLE. For the reasons outlined in our introduction it must become a field of learning in its own right - an integral part of <u>primary</u> education and not a <u>pre-secondary</u> school subject.

7. Part of the Core Curriculum *vs* Optional Activity

Our seventh dichotomy is the least controversial of all. In none of the 5 reports is FLE seen or advocated as an optional activity. The common argument is this:

> If FLE is of such great importance as described above, then it must become part of the core curriculum. If it offers one of the essential education experiences of primary school children, then it has to be included in the obligatory course of studies of all pupils.

The English word "core" is derived from the Latin word <u>cor</u>, meaning "heart". Applied to the curriculum it means those types of experience that are thought to be at the heart of all children's learning in order to help them develop the competences required in their society.

The logic is clear:

Intercultural communicative competence is needed for effective living in our modern society. It can be acquired through foreign language education. Therefore this education has to become part of the core curriculum.

This logic is not new. It is inherent in the works of the protagonists of early foreign language learning from the beginning. H.H. Stern's statement which we quoted in our introduction is a typical example. More arguments of this kind can be found in the utterances of other educationists through the following decades.

The latest statement of this order is the first recommendation of Workshop 8B:

> "In the light of the experience of the workshop participants reported to us from more than 30 countries and the findings of Workshop 4A, 4B and 8A we consider that it is now feasible and desirable for one or more modern languages to be introduced into the primary school curriculum for all children."

Is there any substantial argument for making FLE an optional activity?

The only sustainable argument is that authorities of any democratic country should leave as many educational decisions to the discretion of the parents as possible. If you make FLE part of the core curriculum, you - as a rule - also make it compulsory. Then there is no freedom of choice left for the parents. The children have to take part.

This argument deserves respect, but can also quite easily be contradicted. There is the danger that parents who underestimate the potential of their children shy away from any optional field of learning. They want their children to concentrate on the "really important subjects" and if FLE does not belong to them, these children do not get the chance to participate. Therefore the education authorities of European countries who believe in the importance of foreign language education in primary schools will have to make this education part of the core curriculum of these schools.

Discussion of the seven dichotomies as outlined above reveals the number and nature of the different factors that potentially influence the foreign language learning experience of children, and the foreign language teaching experience of teachers, across Europe. Consideration of these factors at all levels - in the classroom, in the teacher training establishment, in curriculum centres, in the inspectorate and indeed at government level in the member states - will largely determine future action in the field of foreign language education in primary schools. The picture is constantly changing in view of the momentum that FLE at the primary level has achieved, but it remains nonetheless true that there must be a stability of purpose - that of enabling young foreign language learners to enrich and broaden their education during a vital formative period of their schooling, to enhance their cognitive, affective, psychomotor and imaginative capacities, and this within a structured framework, underpinned and permeated by a sound philosophical and pedagogical rationale.

On the basis of the work done at the Council of Europe workshops and the reflections presented in this book, we can finally formulate **eight recommendations** which can be seen as the corner-stones of the successful introduction of foreign languages in the primary sector (age 5/6 to 10/11).

1. Foreign Language Education should become an integral part of primary education in Europe. In order to fulfil their primordial function, namely helping children to acquire the basic competences needed for a full and active participation in society, European primary schools have to include foreign languages and cultures in their curricula (cf. our introduction).

2. The organisation of such FLE will necessarily vary from country to country, but experience has shown that it is particularly successful,

   - if it starts before the age of nine,
   - if it is integrated into the primary curriculum and
   - if it is conducted by well-trained classteachers.

3. As the overall purpose of FLE is considered to be intercultural communicative competence, FLE in primary schools should aim at laying a solid foundation for this competence (cf. Chapter 1).

4. Secondary schools have to build their foreign language teaching on the foundations laid in primary schools, i.e. continuity from the primary to the secondary level must be ensured (cf. Chapter 4).

5. Specific methods have to be used in primary FLE. Above all, they must be child-centred, appropriate to the age of the learners and in accordance with the principles of primary education as a whole (cf. Chapter 2).

6. The existing variety of suitable resources - realia, materials and media - has to be exploited in order to support the learning processes and to make FLE successful (cf. Chapter 3).

7. Programmes and curricula have to be evaluated carefully and their results have to be assessed systematically. Regular evaluation and assessment should become an integral part of FLE in primary schools in order to identify deficiencies and to make modifications and adaptations to meet new educational needs (cf. Chapter 5).

8. A condition of greatest importance for the successful introduction of FLE into the primary schools is the supply of suitably qualified teachers. These teachers have to be experts both in primary education and in foreign language pedagogy. They should gain their qualification through initial studies at colleges and/or universities and through in-service training (cf. Chapter 6).

References

The statements and reflections in this compendium are mainly based on the reports on the five workshops of the Council of Europe mentioned in the introduction:

- *Report on Workshop 4A*. Learning and teaching modern languages in primary schools. Edinburgh, United Kingdom, 2 - 7 June 1991. Compiled and edited by Anthony Giovanazzi.

- *Report on Workshop 4B*. Learning and teaching modern languages in primary schools. Sèvres, France, 12 - 17 December 1993. Compiled and edited by Anne-Marie Kuperberg.

- *Report on Workshop 8A*. Foreign language education in primary schools. Loccum, Germany, 17 - 22 May 1992. Compiled and edited by Peter Doyé and Christoph Edelhoff.

- *Report on Workshop 8B*. Foreign language education in primary schools. Velm, Austria, 7 - 13 May 1995. Compiled and edited by Maria Felberbauer and Dagmar Heindler.

- *Report on Workshop 17*. The challenge of in-service training for foreign language teachers in primary schools. San Lorenzo del Escorial, Spain, 10 - 16 September 1995. Compiled and edited by José Peréz Iruela and Cristina del Moral.

Bibliography

Aebli, H. (1974). Die geistige Entwicklung als Folge von Anlage, Reifung, Umwelt und Erziehungsbedingungen. In Roth, H. (ed.). *Begabung und Lernen.* Stuttgart: Klett, 151-191.

Argondizzo, C. (1992). *Children in Action.* New York: Prentice Hall.

Balbi, R. (1996). *User's Guide for Trainers of Teachers in the Primary School Sector. A Common European Framework of reference for Language Learning and Teaching.* Strasbourg: Council of Europe.

Balbi, B. & Vickery, P. (1990). *Join in.* Rapallo: Cidep.

Balke, G. (1990). *Engelska i Arskurs 5: Resultat fran insamlingen inom den nationella utvaerderingen av grundskolan.* NUengelska 3. Göteborgs Universitet: Institutionen för pedagogik.

Bautz, M. (1988). *Starting English.* NKS-Forlaget.

Bludau, M. (1993). Der frühbeginnende Fremdsprachenunterricht in den Ländern der Bundesrepublik Deutschland. *Neusprachliche Mitteilungen, 46*(2), 74-85.

Böhler, D. (1991). Sprachen und Sprachenlernen. Humboldtsche Perspektiven für Sprachpragmatik. In Brusch, W. and Kahl, P. (eds.). *Europa - Die sprachliche Herausforderung.* Berlin: Cornelsen, 136-150.

Brewster, J., G. Ellis and D. Girard. (1992). *The Primary English Teacher's Guide.* Harmondsworth: Penguin.

Brumfit, C., Moon, J. and R. Tongue (eds.). *Teaching English to children. From practice to Principle.* Collins ELT.

Byram, M. and Zarate, G. (1994). *Definitions, Objectives and Assessment of Socio-cultural Competence.* Strasbourg: Council of Europe.

Campbell, C. and H. Kryszewska. (1992). *Learner-based teaching.* Oxford: Oxford University Press.

Carroll, J.B. (1989). The Carroll Model, a 25-year retrospective and prospective view. *Educational Researcher, 18,* 26-31.

Cohen, R. (1991). Apprendre le plus jeune possible. In: Garabédian, M. (éd.)

Creemers, B.P.M. (1994). *The effective classroom.* London: Cassell.

Cullingford, C. (1989). *The Primary Teacher.* London: Cassell.

Curtain, H. & Pesola, C. (1993) *Languages and children - making the match.* Reading, Mass.: Addison-Wesley.

Doyé, P. (1993). *Fremdsprachenerziehung in der Grundschule.* Zeitschrift für Fremdsprachenforschung, 4(1), 48-90.

Doyé, P. (1995). *Teacher Education.* In Report on Workshop 8B, 133-152.

Doyé, P. (1995a). *La dimension interculturelle de l'apprentissage des langues étrangères - un élement de la formation des enseignants de l'école primaire.* Report on Workshop 17.

Edelenbos, P. (1993). *De aansluiting tussen Engels in het basisonderwijs en Engels in het voortgezet onderwijs.* (Eindrapport SVO-project nr. 0015). Groningen: RION.

Edelenbos, P., & Johnstone, R.M. (Eds). (1996). *Researching Languages at Primary Schools: some European perspectives.* London: CILT.

Edelenbos, P., & Koster, C.J. (1994). Vreemde talen in de Nederlandse basisschool: de stand van zaken in een Europese context. *Tijdschrift voor Onderwijswetenschappen, 24*(1), 14-20.

van Ek, J. (1986). *Objectives for foreign Language Learning*. Volume I: Scope. Strasbourg: Council of Europe.

van Ek, J. (1990). *The Threshold Level*. Strasbourg: Council of Europe.

Ekstrand, L.H. (1979). *Early bilingualism: Theories and Facts*. Lund: University Press.

Ellis, R. (1984). *Understanding Second Language Acquisition*. Oxford: OUP.

Faw, T. and G.S. Belkin. (1980). *Child Psychology*. New York: McGraw-Hill.

Fechner, I. (1992). *Curriculum*. In Report on Workshop 8a, 57-58.

Felberbauer, M. (1991). *Der Englischunterricht an der Grundschule: Ein Beitrag zum interkulturellen Lernen*. Der fremdsprachliche Unterricht, 25 (1), 10-14.

Felberbauer, M. (1993). *English in Austrian Primary Schools*. In Davies Samway, K. and Mc Keon, D. (eds.). Common Threads of Practice TESOL. Alexandria, Va., USA, 86-90.

Freddi, G. (1994). *La lingua straniera alle elementari: materiali de sperimentazione*. London: Longman.

Garabédian, M. (1991). *Enseignement/Apprentissage précoce des langues*. Le Francais dans le Monde: Recherches et Applications. Numéro spécial. Paris.

Gerngross, G. (1995). *Content and Methodology*. In Report on Workshop 8B, 81-87.

Gesell, A. (1956). Developmental trends in language behaviour. *FL Bulletin, 49*, 6-9.

Gritsch, A. (1995). *Continuity in Different Educational Settings*. In Report on Workshop 8B, 101-114.

Halliwell, S. (1992). *Teaching English in the Primary Classroom*. London: Longman.

Hardy, M. et al. (1990). *Studying Child Psychology*. London: Weydenfeld and Nicolson.

Hawkins, E. (1984). *Awareness of Language: An Introduction CUP*.

Holec, H. and I. Huttunen. (1990). *Aspects of Learner Autonomy*. In Biddle, M., P. Malmberg (eds.). Learning to Learn. Investigating Learner Strategies and Learner Autonomy. Primary and Secondary Education and Adult Education. Report on Workshop 2A, Uppsala, December 1990. Strasbourg: Council of Europe, 16-20.

Holt, J. (1984). *How Children Fail*. London: Penguin.

Holt, J. (1984b). *How Children Learn*. London: Penguin.

von Humboldt, W. (1907). *Über die Verschiedenheit des menschlichen Sprachbaues und ihren Einfluß auf die geistige Entwicklung des Menschengeschlechts*. Bd. VII der Gesammelten Schriften. Berlin: Königlich-preußische Akademie der Wissenschaften.

Hurrell, A. (1995). *The Increasing Importance of Foreign Language Learning in the Primary Curriculum*. In Report on Workshop 8B, 69-80.

Hurrell, A. (1995a). *In-service teacher training at primary school level: aims, contents, approaches and strategies*. In Report on Workshop 17.

Hurrell, A. & Satchwell, P. (1996). *Reflections on Modern Languages in Primary Education. Six Case Studies*. CILT.

Huttunen, I., & Kukkonen, L. (1995). *Englannin kielen oppimistuloksia peruskoulun 6. luokan valtakunnallisessa kokeessa 1994*. (Report 22). Helsinki: National Board of Education.

Ilg, F.L. (1956). Childhood and second language learning. *FL Bulletin, 49*, 1-4.

Johnstone, R. (1994). *Teaching modern languages at primary school: Approaches and implications*. (SCRE Publication 121. Practioner MiniPaper 14). Edinburgh: The Scottish Council for Research in Education.

Kelemen, E., & Radnai, Z . (1993). *Read with Roby: Reader and workbook for 7-9*. Budapest: Holnap KKT-OTTV.

Kennedy, C. and J. Jarvis (eds.). (1991). *Ideas and Issues in Primary ELT*. Walton-on-Thames.

Komorowska, H. (1994). *Curriculum development for in-service teacher education in Poland*. Studia Anglica XXVIII, p. 113-122.

Komorowska, H. (1995). *Models and Metaphors in FL Teacher Education. To choose or not to choose*. The Polish Teacher Trainer, no. 5. p. 30-34.

Krashen, S. (1988). *The Natural Approach*. New York: Prentice Hall.

Kubanek-German, A. (1996). Research into primary foreign-language learning in Germany: a trend towards qualitative studies. In P. Edelenbos & R.M. Johnstone (Eds), *Researching Languages at Primary Schools: some European perspectives* (pp. 3-15). London: CILT.

Kuperberg, A.M. (1992). *Continuité*. In Report on Workshop 8A, 67-73.

Larsen-Freeman, D. and Long, M.H. (1990). *An introduction to second language acquisition research*. London and New York: Longman.

Littlewood, W.T. (1983). Contrastive Pragmatics and the foreign Language Learner's personality. In Brumfit, C. (ed.). *Learning and teaching languages for Communication*. London.

Low, L., Brown, S., Johnstone, R., & Pirrie, A. (1995). *Foreign languages in Scottish primary schools - Evaluation of the Scottish Pilot Projects*. (Final Report). Stirling: Scottish CILT.

Low, L., Duffield, J., Brown, S., & Johnstone, R. (1993). *Evaluating foreign languages in Scottish primary schools*. Stirling: Scottish CILT.

Madaus, G., & Kellaghan, T. (1992). Curriculum evaluation and assessment. In P.W. Jackson (Ed.), *Handbook of research on curriculum* (pp. 119-154). MacMillan: New York.

Meyer, E., & Kodron, C. (1993). *Kinder lernen europäische Sprachen e.V.: Jahrbuch 93*. Stuttgart: Ernst Klett Verlag.

O'Neil, Ch. (1993). *Les enfants et l'enseignement des langues étrangères*. CRÉDIF-Hatier/Didier, coll. LAL.

Nias, J., G. Southworth and R. Yeomans. (1989). *Staff Relationships in the Primary School*. London: Cassell.

Page, B. (1993). *Modern Language Teaching/Learning in Secondary Schools in England and Wales*.

Parreren, C. van (1976). *The psychological aspects of the early teaching of modern languages*. IRAL 14, 135-142.

Penfield, W. and Roberts, L. (1959). *Speech and brain mechanisms*. Princeton: University Press.

Phillips, S. (1993). *Young Learners*. Oxford: Oxford University Press.

Piaget, J. (1968). *Le language et la pensée chez l'enfant*. Neuchâtel.

Piepho, H.E. (1992). *A Survey of Approaches*. In Report on Workshop 8A, 46-49.

Pollard, A. and Sarah Tann. (1990). *Reflective Teaching in the Primary School*. London: Cassell.

Radnai, Z. (1990). *The acquisition of English as a foreign language by Hungarian children of 4 to 12 years of age*. Unpublished dissertation, Janus Pannonius University, Pecs.

Radnai, Z. (1994). Productions reflecting processes in Hungarian children's EFL vocabulary acquisition. In G. Bartelt (Ed.), *The dynamics of language processes. Essays in honor of Hans W. Dechert* (pp. 75-83). Tübingen: Gunter Narr Verlag.

Radnai, Z. (1996). English in primary schools in Hungary. In P. Edelenbos & R.M. Johnstone (Eds.), *Researching Languages at Primary Schools: some European perspectives* (pp. 16-26). London: CILT.

Richards, J.C. and D. Nunan. (1990). *Second Language Teacher Education*. Cambridge: Cambridge University Press.

Schimek, F. (1995). *Foreign Languages at Primary Level*. In Report on Workshop 8B, 48-54.

Scott, W. and L. Ytreberg. (1990). *Teaching English to Children*. London: Longman.

Sheils, J. (1993). *Communication in the Modern Language Classroom*. Strasbourg: Council of Europe.

Simpson, M & Ure, J. (1993). *What's the Difference? A Study of Differentiation in Scottish Secondary Schools*. Aberdeen: Northern College.

Stern, H.H. (ed.). (1969). *Languages and the young school child*. London: Oxford University Press.

Taeschner, T. (1990). *A developmental psycholinguistic approach to second language teaching*. New Jersey: Ablex.

Titone, R. (1993). Bilingual education and the development of metalinguistic abilities: a research project. *International Journal of Psycholinguistics, 10*(27), 5-14.

Trim, J. (1995). *The Workshop in the context of the Modern Languages project of the Council of Europe: Modern Languages for European Citizenship*. In Report on Workshop 8B, 34-41.

Vinjé, M.P. (1993). *Balans van het Engels in de basisschool*. Arnhem: CITO.

Vivet, A. (1995). *Sens et rôle des langues dans le développement des enfants*. In Report on Workshop 17.

Wallace, M.J. (1991). *Training Foreign Language Teachers*. Cambridge: Cambridge University Press

Wilson, J. and B. Cowell. (1990). *Children and Discipline*. London: Cassell.

Wingate, J. (1993). *Getting beginners to talk*. New York: Prentice Hall.

Wolff, S. (1981). *Children under Stress*. London: Penguin.

Woodward, T. (1991). *Models and Metophors in Language Teacher Training*. Cambridge: Cambridge University Press.

Wright, A. (1989). *Pictures for language learning*. Cambridge: Cambridge University Press.

Wright, A. (1995). *Storytelling with Children*. Oxford: Oxford University Press.

Profiles of the Contributors

Rita BALBI, a former teacher of English in secondary schools, has been working at IRRSAE Liguria (Istituto Regionale Ricerca Sperimentazione Aggiornamento Educative) since 1984. In that position she has been responsible for the in-service training of teachers of foreign languages in Liguria and has designed and developed the training project for primary school teachers. She has been an animator on four Council of Europe workshops and has worked as consultant for the Council of Europe on various occasions. She is the author of four books and a number of articles concerning the teaching of foreign languages.

Peter DOYÉ is Professor of English at the School of Education, Technische Universität Braunschweig, Germany. In the 1970's he conducted an extensive research project on Primary English in German Schools. He is the author of 6 books and numerous articles on various aspects of foreign language education and co-editor of the "Zeitschrift für Fremdsprachenforschung". He was one of the Directors of Studies at Workshop 8A.

Peter EDELENBOS works as a Senior Researcher for the GION, University of Groningen. After his career in teaching (primary and secondary education) he specialised in research on foreign language teaching in primary schools. At the moment he is engaged in research into the effects of teacher training and the effects of international exchange programmes on pupils and teachers.

Maria FELBERBAUER worked as a teacher in primary and secondary schools before she became a teacher trainer in the Department of English at the Catholic Teacher Training College in Vienna. She was involved in developing foreign language programmes for primary, secondary and special school children and is presently the co-ordinator of the "Lollipop" programme which starts 6-year olds on a foreign language. She has published numerous articles in international language teaching journals and is co-author of publications on methodology and teacher training. She participated in several "New - Style" Workshops on foreign language learning in primary schools and was Director of Studies in Workshop 8B.

Alison HURRELL is currently a lecturer in Modern Languages in Northern College of Education, Aberdeen, Scotland. Prior to that she was a secondary Modern Languages teacher for 22 years. From 1989 - 1992 she was intimately involved as Development Officer in the National Pilot for Modern Languages in the Primary School, helping primary and secondary teachers develop appropriate primary learning contexts and methodologies for the children. Since 1993 she has been working as co-author of the National In-Service Training Programme for primary teachers in French and is at present developing a modular pathway for BEd primary students at Northern College. She has co-authored secondary course books and a Reading Scheme for early learners of French.

Hanna KOMOROWSKA, head of the national committee for language teaching and teacher education reform in Poland in 1989, has been Polish delegate for the Modern Languages Project Group in Strasbourg since 1990. She is the author of several books and numerous articles, her main interests being syllabus design and teacher education. She is Honorary Professor of Thames Valley University in London, professor of applied linguistics at the Instiute of English and the Teacher Training College of English in Warsaw, and Vice-President of Warsaw University.

Manuel TOST PLANET is professor at the Department of French and Romance Philology at the Universitat Autònoma of Barcelona. He lectures in French literature and linguistics, as well as translation. For many years, he has been working in the field of initial and in-service training, taking part in the activities of the Institute of the Science of Education within the same university. He is in charge of the Modern Languages section and, in this context, organises special conferences on the teaching of French. These conferences have now been held for 19 years and attract every year about 500 teachers of all levels of education, coming from all over Spain as well as from other European countries. Finally he coordinates the ADELE Project, a programme of European cooperation sponsored by the LINGUA Bureau in Brussels, in which training and teaching centres from Spain, France, Greece and Portugal cooperate for the production of teaching materials.

Lisbeth HALSE YTREBERG is senior lecturer of English and Elected Rector of Tromsö College, Norway. She has worked as teacher, teacher trainer, college lecturer, and, on various boards and committees, as advisor to the Norwegian Ministry of Education, Research and Church Affairs. She is the author of Engelsk i Grunnskolen (Tano) and co-author of Teaching English to children (Longman).